THE NEW PROFESSIONAL PERSON'S RETIREMENT LIFESTYLE

THE NEW PROFESSIONAL PERSON'S RETIREMENT LIFESTYLE

Jeffrey Webber

For Judy, my wife, without whose support, devotion, and partnership in life would have made it impossible for me to write this book and make this final chapter of our lives so fulfilling.

The quality of life does not depend on happiness alone, but also on what one does to be happy. If one fails to develop goals that give meaning to one's existence, if one does not use the mind to its fullest, then good feelings fulfill just a fraction of the potential we possess...Without dreams, without risks, only a trivial semblance of living can be achieved.

-Mihaly Csikszentmihalyi

Table of Contents

PREFACE

There are at least seventy-six million of us "baby boomers" in the United States born between 1946 and 1964 who are commencing the process of retirement. An important question the professional retiree may be asking himself is, "How will I redefine my life?" According to an AARP Segmentation Analysis, 70% of you feel optimistic about your retirement years, while 28% are very optimistic.

Then, of course, there are those millions already retired who may be bored with mundane activities such as reading the newspaper, watching TV, and eating. However, ennui is not the only problem. Many are fearful of losing their sense of identity and no longer feel stimulated and productive.

Let's face it! You're reading this book because you are either contemplating retirement, in retirement, or simply fantasizing. A significant question that you are grappling with is "What do I do with all of that time?" If you've led a busy, complicated, and sophisticated professional lifestyle, time management becomes even more of an issue. Hopefully, this book will provide you with some answers.

My wife and I are professional retirees. We retired after more than three decades as public school teachers. We had always maintained an active lifestyle. The decision to retire was a long, thought-out, and arduous process to say the least. Part of my indecisiveness in making this decision was due to my relatively young age. I had just turned fifty-five.

Now your reaction to retiring at such a 'childlike' age may echo that of most of my friends and colleagues. The most common reactions reflected thoughts like "what are you crazy? You're too young! You'll go out of your mind!"

Or, "We need you here, you're a good teacher, it won't be the same!" Or, "You're so used to this routine, (the process of getting up and going to work each morning) you won't know what to do with yourself."

I began to think that maybe they were right. Maybe I will not be able to face the uncertainties and challenges that lie ahead: in fact, perhaps the old steadfast routine is the way to go. Furthermore, what about the many friendships I'd cultivated at the workplace? Sometimes in life we get used to doing things a certain way and making change can be difficult and annoying. I may, in fact, need to return to work right away.

I used to joke about the fact that after I retire people will barely remember me, and my accomplishments. In retrospect, people will say "Jeff who? What was his last name?"

As this fourth year of retirement concludes, I can truly say that the separation from that part of my life is almost complete. I have discovered that there is much more to life and the possibilities that await me in my second life excite me with anticipation. I sincerely hope that you will feel the same way after you've read this book.

I've talked to many people who are considering retirement. A major concern, of course, is what to do now. The truth is you need to reinvent yourself. That is, think about what your passions are in life and then pursue them. In effect, your passions can change the world.

I've always felt that a person's major purpose in life must be to positively influence the lives of others. Hence, I became a teacher. Certainly there were many times that I thought I had had enough of the politics, lack of parental support, and all the other disappointments of working as a teacher in an inner-city public school district. But then, as the years progressed, I began to think that even if I changed the lives for the better of a handful of my students, it would be all worth it. And that, my friends, is one of the hopes I have for you as a reader of this book.

Just maybe, as you examine the material in the forthcoming pages, you can find activities that will turn you into a teacher, explorer, or a student, and at the same time, make you feel good about yourself. In the Dalai Lama's book entitled *The Art of Happiness*, he suggests that part of the source of happiness is giving to others.

As previously alluded to in my point about re-inventing yourself, it is hoped that you learn to feel more significant.

We've all felt, at one time or another, that we are somewhat important in the total order of things. Unfortunately, the basis for much of this may have been in the work setting. What you really need to ask yourself is, "What true sense of personal satisfaction did I get from working?" And, "Was this sense of satisfaction long-term?"

I found that personal satisfaction and true self-worth on the job was at best, a temporary feeling. Personal growth, which is enhanced by doing what I really want to do, offers me a true sense of self worth. What I have done, and what is crucial to entering retirement, is to create an entirely new vision for myself. After reading this book, I hope you'll be able to do the same thing.

In order for you to do this, you must have an appropriate mind set. Be prepared to explore new things. This will afford you're the opportunity to receive the greatest benefit from this book. It is insignificant how old you are. I'm fifty-nine years old. You may be eighty. There are resources in this book for everyone. If you've become accustomed to routine, you'll need to break out of that humdrum mode.

INTRODUCTION

Let me make one thing perfectly clear from the outset: The material contained herein is, for the most part, not financial. There is an overabundance of texts that can advise you on financial matters. Hopefully, you've made sense of your financial resources and have a long-term investment plan that will put you in the groove. The AARP analysis that I previously mentioned indicates that two-thirds of baby boomers are satisfied with the amount of money they are putting away.

On the one hand, you may feel somewhat confident that you can afford to retire. Your goal may be to simply pursue passions in life that your busy professional life had precluded you from doing.

On the other hand, there will certainly be those of you who may not wish to retire on a full-time basis. You may simply prefer to lessen your work hours and make life a tad less stressful. Or, you may want to reinvent yourself in terms of another career. Perhaps your interests lie in finding work that suits your passion or true personality. Maybe working keeps you both productive and vital. There's nothing wrong with that. And, of course, depending upon the impact of recent economic times, your retirement nest egg may not be what it was. Perhaps your pension has been reduced or you cannot keep up with the cost of health care. Working may be a necessity. I'll deal with all of this in Chapter 9.

In general, I will be describing a plethora of things for you to do in your retirement. You will be presented with interesting, challenging, and educational activities that you may choose to participate in and services that you may wish to provide or take advantage of. Most of these activities will be consistent with the active and stimulating professional lifestyle you've led. My fondest hope would be to convince those of you who are worried about making this move, to go forward. Remember what I said earlier: It's now time to live for your passions.

An indispensable tool for you to have while reading this book is a computer with Internet access. A study done in 2003 by International Demographics indicates that forty- one percent of people age fifty-five and older regularly go online. Accompanying websites support much of my discussion in the following chapters. (Please note that at the time of this writing websites were all accurate.)

Since I spent a large portion of my career as a Technology Facilitator for a public school system, I really do believe that it does put the world at your fingertips. You'll find that you can tour virtually anywhere in the world, gather information from many libraries, take courses, visit museums, and even buy a car online. If you have no experience with computers, I'll advise you in Chapter 5 of this book on how to learn. And, we'll also discuss interesting things that retirees do with the tools of technology in the same chapter. If I can teach my ninety-year old mother in law how to use a computer, you can learn too.

I recently spent most of a summer and winter traveling around the country with my laptop in hand learning more and more as I traveled. It is important to note that you do not need to spend a lot of money on a system. A basic system for under $1000 will readily do the job. If you cannot afford the cost of a computer, or simply do not wish to purchase one, proceed to your local library. There you should have access to an Internet ready machine. These days, most libraries have high-speed access. Since time restrictions may apply, it's best to have a list of the websites you want to visit in hand.

Back in 1946, the first computer produced was 150 feet wide. Things have changed quite a bit since 1946, the beginning of the boomer age. The television age began that year with the DuMont Television Network making its own TV. A twenty-inch TV would have cost you $2500 back then. It was certainly a rich person's pleasure. But, by 1953 production had risen to seven million per year. So, the television became a major passion and continues to be the fastest growing bit of technology through all time.

This book will provide you, as a retired professional, with ideas that should meet your needs no matter what your financial capabilities are. That is, whether you have a limited income, or are quite comfortable, even if you need to work, information is the following chapters will assist you in forming a solid foundation to experience a more satisfying retirement.

CHAPTER 1: READY . . .SET . . .G0!

In order to make this book work for you, you'll need to take stock of yourself and engage in some self-analysis to determine what you would really like to do during retirement. Above all, be truthful and do not fantasize unless you are prepared to make those fantasies a reality.

For example, if you're thinking that you'd really like to learn to repair your own car, but you cannot recognize which end of a wrench is which, or, if you abhor grease and dirt, and you have very little patience, perhaps this idea needs reconsideration.

McCants and Robert, in their book entitled *Retire To Fun and Freedom*, suggest that you list your strengths in the following terms:

1. Things I do very well
2. Things I do moderately well
3. Character strengths
4. Personality strengths
5. Things that I would like to do better

They also recommend that you consider how important the following are to you: love, respect, and money. Further, you should ask yourself what you like and dislike most about your present life, as well as what you do for pleasure, and which of your skills gives you the most satisfaction.

Ultimately, it is important to come up with a plan. If you've led a rigorous lifestyle prior to retirement, and suddenly you are faced with a perplexing lack of activity, you may become quickly disillusioned. This plan is a course of action that you will definitely follow. By it's own nature, the plan must be long term, as it will effect a change in your routine lifestyle. Please understand that since retirement will begin a new period in your life, the process of plan development may be somewhat experimental. I suggest that your actual plan be developed at the conclusion of your reading this book.

Try to follow these steps as you develop your plan:

* Start simply - Remember: If you are new to retirement, it's best to work out a

schedule that won't overburden you.

* Balance your life - Strike a balance between your household activities and chores and your recreational life. Above all, your eventual goal here is to feel a deep sense of satisfaction.

* Do what you really want - Don't be afraid to experiment with new ideas. If you've always wanted to

write, take that course on creative writing either at a local college, or as part of the adult education program in your town, or as an arm of your local senior citizen center if you are in the appropriate age bracket.

In his book, *The Joy of Not Working*, Ernie Zelinkski suggests that you develop a Leisure Tree entitled "Options For My Leisure." Basically, the development of this tree is rooted in four important ideas:

1. Leisure activities that turn you on now
2. Leisure activities that have turned you on in the past
3. New leisure activities you have considered doing
4. Activities that will get me physically fit

You may even want to turn your leisure tree into a retirement tree, perhaps renaming it "Options For My Retirement". This would afford you the opportunity to visualize the broader perspective of your life, particularly if you are planning to work part time or volunteer in a work related situation.

A major benefit of developing a plan in this fashion is that it allows you to group your ideas in an easy to read, compact format. In addition to the basic leisure tree, an enhanced leisure (or retirement) tree can be developed from which you can capitalize on one component such as travel activities. This will make the prioritization process more efficient. You will most likely come up with a large number of activities at the outset. Indeed, this type of plan development will assist you in brainstorming ideas, which you will hopefully retrieve from reading this book.

In her book entitled *Retiring as a Career, Making the Most of Your Retirement*, Betsy Kyte Newman presents an even simpler way to chart your activities. She calls it a "Retirement Life Grid Form". Here is an abbreviated example:

Activity   Time (hours per month)   Benefit   Related to Plan

_____

_____

_____

_____

_____

Really Getting Ready

As you know by now, getting ready to make that big move into the next phase of your life requires much more than financial preparedness. According to Alison Sommers, a retirement life planning coach for The Drake Group, "you need to have a purpose in retirement - even if it's to play golf."

Sommers guides her clients through a comprehensive "Retirement Success Profile" © which measures a client's readiness to retire in fifteen critical areas. A variety of factors should be considered. These include:

*Directedness: setting your purpose in life on your own

*Work Reorientation: replacing the benefits (money, time management, purpose, status, and socialization) you receive from working

*Attitude: what you anticipate your life will be like after in the future

*Health Perception: your evaluation of your own state of health

*Life Stage Satisfaction: the degree to which you find your present life fulfilling

*Dependents: your level of freedom from the burden of care-giving responsibilities

*Family and Relationships: how much satisfaction you derive from marital or family life

Be Creative

Dr. Gene Cohen, M.D., Ph.D., of George Washington University defines creativity as "bringing something new into existence that's valued." He suggests that you create a social portfolio of lifetime social and artistic activities. This "portfolio" should be comprised of a mix of individual and group activities with varying energy and mobility requirements. The following suggestions are from his book, *The Creative Age: Awakening Human Potential in the Second Half of Life:*

1. Group activities/high energy - Make a list of activities for when you are feeling energetic and social.
2. Individual activities/high energy - List things you can do on your own.
3. Group activities/low energy - How about starting a family newspaper or neighborhood book club?
4. Individual activities/low energy - Create a family tree or a collection of family recipes.

When my wife and I retired, we soon realized that part of our plan that really works for us was to have something to look forward to each morning. So, we bought kayaks and a tandem bicycle, we took tennis lessons, golf lessons and we hike more frequently. These are great activities when the weather cooperates. For times when the weather is inappropriate, my wife joined a gym and I joined an indoor swimming club. So, that is how we start each day.

You really want your retirement to be successful and your experiences to be positive. Obviously, there will be trial and error in finding activities that you really do enjoy. Certainly though, you can give yourself a head start.

Another very important goal that you must set for yourself is to physically get in shape (see Chapter 2). This is crucial to maintaining a high level of mental acuity, as well being able to physically carry out the plan that you have developed for yourself. Since you may have lessened your levels of activity after retirement this goal becomes even more pronounced. If you have not done so in a long while, make certain that you get a complete physical examination before you implement your plan, especially if vigorous activities are included. Of course, it is crucial for you as part of this plan, to follow good dietary habits as well.

If you have that computer that I recommended that you obtain, log on to the wonderful AARP website (*aarp.org*) and go the health guide link (*aarp.org/healthguide*). There, you'll find great tips for maintaining a good diet, keeping fit, as well as the most recent health discoveries. There is also information on developing that perfect body and tips for saving your heart as well as an abundance of other health related links. Also, check out their health and wellness guide. (*aarp.org/health/*).

It is important to note here that you really should join AARP. Their scope over the years has broadened greatly to meet the needs of baby boomers like you and I. In earlier years their appeal was mainly geared towards less active retirees. These days, they are very involved in various pieces of legislation that will have a pronounced effect on our future such as prescription drugs and retiree health benefits. For many years, AARP has been urging Congress to come up with equitable solutions for retirees' health benefits that address the escalating costs of this care. Remember, that you only need to be fifty years old to join. And, you'll be amazed at all of the discounts that come with membership including hotels and tourist attractions.

Recent statistics indicate that seventy percent of seniors go online for the purpose of checking out the wide variety of health care websites (See the Website Directory of this book for suggestions). They research symptoms of illnesses and diseases and look for suggested medical procedures. The URAC (Washington based health care accrediting organization) suggests that you log onto their website (*webapps.urac.org/websiteaccreditation/default.htm*) to examine their recommendations for quality health care sites.

One of the biggest challenges one faces upon retirement is what to do during the day. Many activities are based on evening participation. At first glance, it seems that unless you're a senior citizen and belong to a senior citizen center, there's nothing to do. Well, I've just turned fifty-eight, am very active, and am not ready to settle down to a life of bingo and sing-a-longs. Maybe you feel the same way that I do. That said, my research leads me to believe that you'll be amazed at what is available for you both day and night.

Financial Independence

How often have we thought about the advantages of being independently wealthy? Would it not be great to formulate your retirement plan with no consideration as to cost?

Since many of us are nowhere near that point, I do have another suggestion to encourage financial independence.

If you are challenged by and need help with your personal finances, you can bring a daily money manager on board. These specialists can be volunteers or paid on an hourly basis. Either way, their job is to help keep your finances on track. And, of course, this move may be of great help to you in developing that retirement plan, which you are definitely going to follow.

With so many baby boomers reaching retirement age, demand for these services is growing. Basically, money managers ensure that your bills are paid, bank accounts dealt with, and checkbooks balanced. They'll also organize your tax records and even deal with insurance companies.

The important point to remember here is that if you think you need help, don't be afraid to acknowledge it. Volunteers may readily be available through local senior services. If you live in the Dallas area, contact Senior Source (*scgd.org*) for information on volunteer money managers.

If you can afford to pay a professional money manager for services rates may range from twenty-five dollars per hour. Log onto the American Association of Daily Money Managers website (*aadmm.com*) for a description of the services provided as well as assistance in locating a manager.

You should also note that some local governments have reduced fee or free services. You can also contact AARP (202-434-2143) for additional information.

"Hone" Your Driving Skills

As you prepare to face the challenges that lie ahead in this new phase of your life, and to make certain that you can be as active as possible and follow suggestions made in this book, you may need to think about transportation issues.

If you do not currently drive, and you have transportation venues arranged, then you are in great shape. Perhaps you reside in a community that offers transportation, or maybe you are taking advantage of a senior ride program.

Assuming that you are a licensed driver, it is important to consider staying safely on the road for as long as possible. You should know that older drivers have advocates such as the American Automobile Association (AAA) and American

Association of Retired Persons (AARP). They argue that the emphasis should not be on taking older drivers off the road, but on helping them drive more safely. It is interesting to note that there are currently at least 18.5 million licensed drivers who are seventy-one or older.

The National Highway and Safety Administration (*nhtsa.dot.gov /people/ injury/ olddrive*) recommends that you continually assess any physical changes you experience that may affect your driving skills. Of particular concern are declining vision, stamina, general physical fitness and reaction times. At their website you can find very informative article entitled "Driving Safely While Aging Gracefully". Along with areas of concern they suggest ways to get help and methods of alternative transportation.

The AARP Driver Safety Program (*aarp.org/life/drive*)(888-227-7669) is an excellent way for you to achieve the aforementioned goal of staying safely on the road for as long as possible. It is an eight-hour course specially designed refresher course for drivers aged fifty and beyond. It only costs ten dollars and there are no tests involved. The course teaches participants to sharpen defensive driving skills and refine other existing skills. Many states even mandate a multi-year discount on automobile insurance upon successful completion of the course. The curriculum includes topics such as vision and hearing changes, reaction time changes, effects of medication, and hazardous driving situations. At the website you can search for a class near you by typing in your zip code.

AARP offers an excellent array of driver safety pamphlets to help you learn more about this important subject. You can also test your driver IQ with a multiple- choice test about driving techniques. There are additional links at the site that lead to pages of driving safety tips.

Seniordrivers.org is a website hosted by Lon and Myra Kramer who are senior drivers. Their purpose is to keep you driving safely for as long as possible by improving your skills behind the wheel. The site is rich in driving tips with lots of pictures and videos in a simple, easy to follow format. Driving links include "fitness", "getting ready", "driving", "travel links", "emergencies", and even a quiz.

By the way, driver rehabilitation specialists say that there are a variety of ways you can make driving safer:

- Corrective mirrors - these wider mirrors may help to reduce blind spots

- Raised driver seats - a seat cushion can restore lost ground
- Pedal extensions - can be a great help to shorter drivers
- Reduction of distractions - to help you focus you may need to keep the radio turned off along with curtailing conversations

CHAPTER 2: DAY ONE-LET'S GET IN SHAPE

With all the hype, you should realize by now that it is important (especially at our age) to engage in some physical activity on a frequent basis.

Recent research from the Centers for Disease Control and Prevention points to the fact that half of American retirees are completely sedentary. A common misconception these days is that when you are sixty or sixty-five years old, it's too late to begin exercising. Well folks, many experts agree that exercise for seniors can produce a variety of benefits. Those benefits include increased endurance, increased strength (allowing seniors to be more independent), better balance, and more flexibility of the muscles. All of these benefits can slow down certain aspects of aging.

Before you go out and buy an expensive set of weights and barbells, there is another important consideration for you to ponder. Experts also agree that as we age, it is easier to get injured and it takes longer to heal sprains and strains. As you may be aware, physical changes and ailments that accompany advancing age include loss of muscle mass, decreased bone density, diminished muscle and tendon flexibility, and joints less able to handle impact. Your basic goal here may be to get into top physical without over doing the process.

As previously indicated, it is vital for you to get an examination before you begin any program of sustained physical activity, particularly if you've not exercised before. If you are one of these people, check out Active Living Every Day (*activeliving.info*). Online courses are offered by the Cooper Clinic and Brown University to help sedentary people become active.

So, here are some choices for you to get in shape.

Swimming

When you think about it, water really does offer a variety of benefits to keep you healthy. If you are looking for a low impact exercise, supported by a natural resistance, aquatic exercise may be for you. And, you will be surrounded by the soothing nature of water, which has proven to relieve day-to-day stress.

Each morning when the weather is either too cold to do much outside, or inclement in general, I swim. I prefer to swim laps as opposed to taking classes. You'll find those choices available to you as well at most indoor pool facilities.

During the fall, winter, and spring months, I belong to a seasonal pool club called the Aquadome. This program is sponsored by a local non-profit foundation. They rent the pool from a local club. The heated pool is covered by a dome and works wonderfully as an indoor facility for the cold weather months. The benefits from this form of cardio-vascular exercise are great.

Participants in water aerobics exercise classes use weights and equipment in combination with the resistance of the water. This leads to a highly effective workout for the entire body. Indeed, this workout builds strength, stamina, and flexibility. Types of exercises include jogging, stretching, and cross-country skiing. Activity levels begin at the low intensity stage and proceed through mid intensity to the high intensity workout. If you would like further information about water aerobics log onto the home page of the Aquatic Exercise Association (*aeawave.com*).

Many pool clubs also offer arthritis aquatic exercise that is based on the Arthritis Foundation Aquatic Program. The approach here is designed to maintain and increase flexibility and range of movement. These classes are ideal for individuals who are restricted from participating in land-based programs due to various physical restrictions such as arthritis and back ailments or hip replacements. Remember that this is a low impact exercise approach that works well for individuals of all fitness levels. By the way, I've been told that most facilities also offer personal aquatic training with a personal trainer that can work towards your specific goals which might include improving muscle tone and stress reduction.

Participants that I interviewed for this book report tremendous gains in their health as a result of the swimming. Cholesterol levels have been dramatically reduced and general overall feelings of health have improved. A few people have indicated that they no longer need the help of assistive devices such as canes and crutches. Better sleeping habits are noted, as is improved mental alertness.

You can also contact your local YMCA (*www.ymca.org*) for available swimming opportunities. The "Y" often rents space at hotel pools. Further, many of these same hotels have their own pool clubs. Most Holiday Inns (*holiday-inn.com*) or Holiday Inn Express hotels do this. You can also check with local heath clubs or even your own local recreation center. If you really feel adventurous, you can swim with dolphins (*dolpindiscovery.com, discoverycove.com*). Of course, if you are one of the lucky people who live in a warm climate, looking for an indoor facility may be unnecessary. One important consideration to help you along with this: The AMA (American Medical Association) feels that swimming is one of the best choices for a low impact cardiovascular exercise. For more information about the benefits of swimming, go to swimming.about.com.

Join a Gym, a Public Recreation Program, or the YMCA

Gyms and health clubs abound in most cities and towns nowadays. Researchers say that the fastest growing segment of the fitness industry are adults over the age of fifty-five. Club memberships for this group are up more than 350% since 1987.

Deciding which one to join may not, however, be as difficult as you think. If you like to work out like a "sweat hog" on your own, there are usually many choices. If you prefer a planned thirty-minute workout, then you'll need to focus in that direction. Curves for Women (*curvesinternational*.com) offers an excellent choice here, and memberships are honored at over 1700 Curves facilities around the country. They focus on strength training with aerobic exercise in a comfortable environment and as of this date the charge is only thirty-two dollars per month for unlimited use. World Gym (*worldgym.com*) offers a program for just about anyone.

You should also check with your local Recreation Department. Most towns and cities offer a variety of fitness programs as part of their Recreation Departments or Adult Education Programs. You'll most likely find a variety of aerobic activities including exercise classes, tennis, and swimming. Most likely, you will be in groups with people just like yourself.

Once again, by all means visit in person or online your local YMCA branch for additional activities. If you have the capability to do so, visit their wonderful website to link to their local branch. There, you can explore all related groups.

The Importance of Weight Training

Medical experts agree that it is really never to late when it comes to weight training. The benefits to seniors are quite real.

With regular training (twice per week) you can count on stronger bones (especially important in women), improved posture and balance, and maybe even an easier time accomplishing your daily tasks. Don't think that we are talking about pumping heavy iron here. You can enjoy the benefits by buying some simple equipment or joining a gym.

Other benefits include burning calories and developing more muscle mass.

A study at University of Alabama concluded that non-athletic women ages sixty to seventy-seven that began regular weight training made dramatic gains in strength and walking speed.

Experts say that two thirty to sixty minute sessions a week are good for beginners. You may want to begin the process by signing up for a class in weight training. They also suggest that you can keep the cost of equipment down by either joining a gym (short-term) or by buying some inexpensive home equipment such as hand weights for as little as three dollars. You can also purchase resistance bands for about ten dollars. The idea here is to see if you like it before you spend the additional money.

Workout at Home

If you prefer a less structured workout, and would rather not be confronted with spandex laced sweaty bodies, then clearly this is your choice. The important consideration here is that you need to make certain that you exercise on a regular basis. Remember: After you've had that physical examination, you can feel confident about doing this. It is, however, important to know your limitations and not overdo it.

Getting on the treadmill or stationary bicycle has to become second nature to you. You can find an excellent selection of equipment at your local department stores such as Sears, or you local sporting goods store. Give yourself a good twenty-minute workout each day.

Walk, Speed Walk, Run

While I was working, I would speed walk each day during my lunch hour. I'm sure you've probably seen the likes of people like me doing this, especially if you are in a city. This aerobic activity lasted about a half hour and worked very well for me. Now that I'm retired, I still do a comparable walk each day when I don't bike or hike. Recent recommendations from medical experts such as the University of Connecticut Medical Center suggest that even a thirty minute walk around the local park, three days a week at a brisk pace will do the trick. Again, you don't need to overdue it. Many seniors take regular, brisk walks at the local shopping mall. This is especially satisfying on those cold days. You can even stop in at the local ice cream store for a quick break!

If you run, make certain that you've got good running shoes that will provide you with the appropriate support and that you are in reasonably good physical condition.

Bike

I love to bike. Depending on where you live this could be an all year round activity. In 1995, my wife and I purchased a used tandem bicycle. If you have someone to share this experience this with, I highly recommend it. Not only is a great bonding activity, it 's great to be able to share the sights and general travel experiences. Recently, we bought a new folding tandem that will accompany us when we travel overseas. As with any physical activity, you'll need to be in somewhat good physical condition. Otherwise, the captain (person in front) will end by peddling for the person in back (stoker) or vice versa. We love to bike the Back Bay National Wildlife Refuge in Virginia. Weather you bike on a single or tandem, trails like this are truly magnificent. You bike among the wild horses, deer, and other wildlife. This particular trail ended up at the ocean, much to our delight.

Many bike trail publications are available on either a state-by-state, regional, national, or national park basis. Good examples, *Best Bike Paths of New England* and *Best Bike Paths of the Southwest* by Wendy Williams (Simon and Schuster) describe in detail the trails, their levels of difficulty, and conditions. A good source for these publications is *amazon.com*. This website reviews and rates all related material. If you are a camper, as we are, then you may have available to you the best of many worlds. Many of our state, National Park, and public campgrounds, offer the camper great biking (or hiking) trails either on premises or nearby. You can get further information from the National Parks website (*nps.gov*) from Valeria (*rvamerica.com*), or from your state site which may offer a bicycle trail link.

And, of course, you can simply ride your bike in your own neighborhood to get your dose of good, low impact, aerobic exercise. If you live in a colder climate, you can bring your bike indoors and mount the rear wheel on a special stand, which allows you to continue to ride on a stationary basis. Further, there is always the stationary bike at the gym.

For additional information on some really cool bicycle vacations see Chapter 7 on Bicycle Touring.

Hike

Let's assume that you arc the type of person that loves the outdoors. Let's also assume that you are in reasonably good physical condition. Perhaps you've decided that going for a walk is not stimulating enough. Well then, the answer is simple. Why not go for a hike and get the advantages of both getting your exercise and learning at the same time. There is so much to learn and observe about our environment.

Now don't become apprehensive and think to yourself "hiking is for muscle people". You can begin by taking a very simple leisurely hike and then increase the level of challenge gradually. My mother-in-law hiked until she was eighty years old. When she was sixty-three years old she climbed a three thousand foot mountain in New Hampshire.

There are hikes for people of all levels of abilities. You can walk a simple nature trail at a local nature center or take an easy hike at a public garden center. Or, you can just as easily take a hike at the nearest state or public park.

I recommend that you always carry with you the following three things: a trail map (if you hike in a network of trails), water, and cell phone, if you have one.

In Connecticut, many towns have created walking trails. Contact your town or city hall to ascertain that information. Also, most state websites have information and links to hiking facilities. Make certain that you check out the GORP (Great Outdoor Recreation Pages) website (*www.gorp.com*). This is a great hiking resource that includes clickable maps of where to hike, as well as discussions about gear and all of the essentials.

Speaking of websites, if you live in New England, I suggest that you check out the Appalachian Club site (*www.outdoors.org*), or better yet, buy their guide.

The *Falcon Guides* (published by the Globe-Pequot Press) series is an excellent source for hiking locations around the country. They have easy to understand and very descriptive guides available for most states and major attractions. They will even help you with information on where to park your vehicle.

By the way, make sure you carry your National Audubon Society's North American Birds Book and their great book entitled North American Trees in your backpack. As I mentioned earlier, there's a lot to learn about the wonders of nature.

Walking the World sponsors walking vacations. Read more in Chapter 7.

Paddle

For those of you not familiar with the term *paddling*, let's get one thing perfectly straight. I'm not talking about anything to do with ducks or fraternity initiations. I'm referring to the wonderful sports of canoeing, kayaking, or boating.

When I retired, I bought two small lightweight (35lbs) kayaks. The significant considerations for persons of our age doing something like this all revolve around ease of use. Unless you use your watercraft in only one location (where you can store it), ease of transport becomes of paramount importance. My wife and I travel to a variety of locations to kayak since we are able to maneuver our boats. If you are not up to the physical requirements of doing this, you can easily rent kayaks, canoes, or rowboats at most lakes and recreation areas. Remember that all-important source for finding these areas is your state website.

So, if you're going to transport, I recommend that you use a low profile car with an easy mount roof rack (Thule makes a great rack that is easy to use). Or, if you have a van, SUV, or pick up truck, then your craft can be transported inside.

Make certain that your boats are lightweight. This may become more difficult if you decide to canoe, as they can be on the heavy side, particularly if you select fiberglass composition.

On the other hand, there are several companies that sell inflatable canoes and kayaks. Seacraft (*seacraft.com*) Company offers a variety of these that are easy to both inflate and deflate and are quite safe. As of this writing their prices begin at about three hundred dollars.

As far as where to boat, go to your local bookstore and pick up a guide. If you are fortunate enough to live close to lakes or rivers, as we do, then you have local resources.

In terms of beneficial exercise, the gains from this that you will receive will come mostly in the form of upper body strength. The muscles in your arms will become more developed.

Again, these sports have the added benefit of allowing you to learn about and be a part of our beautiful natural environment, and they are activities that persons of our age can readily participate in.

Yoga

This popular method of conditioning is relatively low impact, meditative, and less stressful than other forms of exercise. Many programs are offered at local recreation departments, and adult education programs. You can also check out two wonderful websites that can be great resources for you. First, *www.yogasite.com* offers a comprehensive directory of retreats, teachers, and postures. Second, *www.yogajournal.com* will keep you abreast of latest techniques. Also, don't forget your local library.

Tai Chi

I spent most of my years as an educator at a school, which was located within the Yale University community. A large Asian population resided in this metropolitan area. On many a morning, I observed groups of Asian people practicing a series of slow, balancing movements on the front lawn of our school. These movements included arms waving in slow and graceful motions. It was some time before I realized that I was observing the ancient practice of Tai Chi, an exercise for all ages, developed by Buddhist monks around the thirteenth century.

Tai Chi does not increase respiratory rates, as does other cardio-vascular exercises. Rather, its choreographed motions resemble a combination of stretching and dancing. Immediate benefits from this exercise include relaxation of the body and mind, improvement in breathing, and perhaps even greater mobility. As a senior, you may realize relief from arthritic pain and a reduction in stress. Additionally, it's not too strenuous nor does it require any costly equipment. Tai Chi can be practiced in a group or individually.

You should be able to find instruction information at senior citizen centers, martial arts schools, the local YMCA, as well as the old faithful, your local adult education program. If you log onto www.taichi.com you'll find a number of great videos.

Other Ideas

Even the most basic exercise can improve your overall energy levels and stamina. Some suggestions here include:

* Go shopping at a mall.
* Take the stairs rather than the elevator or escalator.
* Park you car farther away in parking lots.
* If you play golf, consider walking rather than riding in a cart.

CHAPTER 3: KEEP THE BRAIN CELLS ACTIVE

I recently read a story in the local newspaper about a ninety-year old gentleman who received an undergraduate degree from a university. I've always imagined that when (and if) I reach that age, I would have other things on my mind, assuming of course that I still had much of a mind left.

Then I examined the newest research, which suggested that keeping that "gray matter " active, in conjunction with physical exercise, is a key to a long, healthy, and mentally acute life.

I care for an uncle who is ninety-seven. He lives by himself and for the most part, does not heed any of my suggestions regarding physical health or diet. I was amazed to find out that a hobby that he has had for years may have had a pronounced effect on why he continues to be so sharp intellectually. On a daily basis he does crossword puzzles. He has been doing this for at least twenty years. His doctor feels that in combination with reading newspapers and magazines, he may have avoided the inevitable cognitive decline that is associated with aging.

Check out these facts: William Paley was still running CBS at eighty-nine. Picasso turned out 140 canvasses when he was eighty-eight and was still painting when he died at ninety-two.

Dr. David Bennett, director or the Rush Alzheimer's disease Center in Chicago, looked at 700 elderly, dementia free nuns, priests and brothers. They were questioned about their various activities. Those activities included reading, doing crossword puzzles, and going to museums. Most of these activities were found to protect against Alzheimer's and resulted in lower rates of decline in short term memory and perceptual memory (a persons ability to perceive new information.) He concluded that doing a variety of different enrichment things stimulates different parts of the brain.

I really do believe in the old adage "you're never too old to learn something new". Over the years as a public school teacher, I had many occasions to work with the local public and private colleges and universities in the area. Much to my delight, I observed many retired people taking courses. In fact, many are actually working towards a degree matriculation.

As a retired professional person, you may have at least one college degree. Perhaps you've been taking courses (for business or pleasure) for a number of years.

One of the newest and fastest growing retirement trends are retirement communities opening on or near college campuses. Retirees are drawn by the flurry of activities in college towns.

They relish the chance to continue learning while living along side like-minded adults. People who live in these communities are looking for something more intellectually stimulating in their daily lives. I'll discuss this in more detail in Chapter 8 - Finding a New Place to Live.

There are many types of course offerings available to you, if you are interested. Let's first begin with a reminder about a prerequisite that I consider to be very important.

You Really Do Need Those Technology Skills

Did you acquire that computer yet that I recommended in the introduction of this book? You knew I was going to bring this up again given my background as a public school computer educator.

If you are not yet computer literate, or, if you are afraid to turn on your computer, it's time to get busy and learn. Let's face it. We are in an age of ever changing digital technological advancement. All of these changes will certainly bring the world closer to your doorstep (or should I say desktop) and allow you to broadly expand your communication with that outside world.

As previously alluded to, I've spent many years as a public school computer educator working with urban students. Many of these kids will never leave the inner city. Many of their lives changed dramatically with the arrival of the Internet. They've learned to write better and communicate effectively with students from foreign countries and, in fact, "virtually" visited many of these countries. The students worked closely with age appropriate peers on common projects related to world issues. They also visited museums, gathered information from libraries, studied the weather, worked on art projects, learned to creatively write, and improved typing skills.

Why am I telling all of this? The simple truth is that if they could do it, so can you. It's much easier than you think. More details on this in Chapter 4.

Adult Education

By all means, contact your local board of education to determine if adult education programs are offered in your community. You'll find the cost to be minimal, the offerings to be extensive, and the rewards to be quite satisfying. Many communities offer joint programs in conjunction with neighboring towns and cities. By pooling resources, these towns and cities are readily able to expand their course offerings. Most courses are offered in the evening from 7:00PM - 9:00PM. A semester typically lasts four to six weeks.

A recent sampling of district courses in the State of Connecticut include the following:

- All aspects of financial planning
- All aspects of computer operations and associated software
- Weaving
- Creative writing
- Auto repair
- Ballroom dancing
- Golf lessons
- Tennis lessons
- Chinese cooking
- Italian cooking
- Vegetarian cooking
- Seamanship
- Yoga
- CPR
- Reading classic novels

- Candle making
- Foreign language basic conversation

Local senior citizen center, recreation center, and YMCA

If you are a person that would prefer to engage in learning activities during the day, then you should obtain a schedule of events from your local senior citizen center or recreation center. Don't be apprehensive about doing this because you feel that you're too young. In my town, the minimum age for joining the recreation center senior activities is fifty. You'll find that the events are varied and reasonably priced. Most centers offer great deals on day trips to tourist attractions, day classes of general interest, and lessons sports.

Let's not forget that wonderful local resource, the YMCA. You can get a very precise idea about what's being offered when you log onto their website (*www.ymca.org*). The main site has links to their twenty four hundred branches around the country. From there, you can click on programs offered at each branch.

Go Back to School!

How About Graduate School?

Now that we're living longer and healthier lives, it may be easier to begin a new and enriching life cycle. If your nest is empty, and you have the desire to continue learning, why not go back to school? According to Department of Education, 120,000 men and women over the age of fifty are earning graduate degrees.

With the increase in longevity, comes a distinct difference from previous generations when the emphasis was closing down when you were in your sixties. For this generation of retirees we look forward to opening up. Or, as I've previously mentioned a thousand times, reinventing ourselves.

Neuropsychology experts say that although you may experience a decrease in the speed of learning, the brain benefits from increased activity and may, in fact, extend your life just as effectively as physical exercise.

Remember, if you want to continue working at something new, education may be the key to your next career.

Most public colleges and universities will allow you to take courses without being enrolled in a planned program working towards a degree. At many locations, you can even take courses for free, if you are a senior citizen. If you live near a community college, you can do the same thing. You may find that the courses offered are of a broader nature. You might also consider going back to college and working towards that degree you've always wanted.

A relatively new way of taking courses is called distance learning. You don't actually go to classes. You become part of a rapidly growing roster of virtual campuses. You do all of your coursework at home on your computer through the Internet. Online schools offer programs that lead to a bachelor's degree, master's degree, and doctor of philosophy. Many public and private colleges and universities offer distance-learning programs. The University of Phoenix (*uoponline.com*) offers a wide variety of degrees with full accreditation. That institution is very highly rated by the Wall Street Journal. You can choose from programs in business, criminal justice, education, healthcare, and technology.

You can also take courses for pleasure. These are wonderful opportunities for those of us who do not wish to travel the hectic roads in all kinds of inclement weather. The important consideration here is that you must have the appropriate technology available to you to do this. If you do not have a home computer you may be able to borrow one, or, perhaps you can use one at your public library. If you are retired, this is a wonderful opportunity that will certainly save you both time and money and avail you of excellent educational opportunities.

A discussion of online programs in art can be found in Chapter 5 (Hobbies) under the art section.

One terrific resource is Yahoo Distance Learning (*yahoo.com/Education/Distance_Learning*). A great example of the variety of programs offered is the Connecticut Distance Learning Consortium (*www.ctdlc.org*). I've found that most states offer distance-learning networks that will explain in great detail which courses are available in your area.

A word of caution is justified at this time. If you would like to matriculate towards a college degree, make sure that the institution you are thinking of dealing with is both legitimate and accredited. According to Susan Reilly, director of accreditation with the Distance Education and Training Council in Washington, many programs have no real credentials whatsoever. There are also non-accredited institutions that are legitimate. She suggests that online offerings from prominent universities are virtually guaranteed to be real. That office examines curricula and does a thorough review. Work is probably the most revealing quality of an online university or college. "If you don't have to work to earn something it's probably not legitimate," says Reilly. She recommends the following three books as some of the best references about online education.

1. *Peterson's Guide to Distance Learning Programs*

2. *Thorsen's Guide to Campus Free College Degrees*

3. *The Best Distance Learning Schools (from GetEducated.Com)*

So, if you really have a desire to further your education, or you're just simply interested in learning more about a topic, there's really no reason why you can't.

Institute For Retired Professionals

(nsu.newschool.edu/irp)

If you reside in the New York area, consider joining the IRP. Members learn and explore freely without exams and grades. They take learning quite seriously. Students range in age from fifty-six to ninety-one. The program began in an effort to provide and intellectual challenge for professional retirees.

The curriculum is comprised of various study groups and workshops. The heart of the program is peer learning. Study groups are offered in art, drama, history, literature, music, politics, science, and current affairs. Classes are held at the New School, located in Greenwich Village, New York. Current examples of study groups include Great Poets, Contemporary Fiction, Great American Songwriters, Biotechnology, and the World of Mozart. You can contact the school at 212-229-5682.

Elderhostel

Elderhostel is America's first and the worlds largest educational travel organization for adults fifty-five years of age and older. They are a non-profit organization that provides exceptional learning adventures in more than one hundred countries around the world. Over ten thousand programs are offered a year. In 2000, two hundred fifty thousand people took advantage of the programs that are offered.

Participants in these programs come from every walk of life to learn together and seek a richer understanding of subjects ranging from the ecology of Madagascar to the plays of William Shakespeare. The faculty includes university professors, noted academic specialists, museum professionals, and local scholars.

Lectures are complimented by field trips and cultural excursions that provide a close up look at the lecture topics. In addition, all travel details are attended to and are included in the fee. Elderhostel programs issue no homework and there are no tests or grades. The goals include the chance to broaden your mind, enrich your life, and share new experiences.

Past Elderhostel learning experiences include:

- exploration of America's greatest music on a Mississippi River paddleboat that visits cities from Memphis to New Orleans
- studies of Indian history and culture while visiting ancient forts, temples, and palaces from Delhi to Jaipur to Jodhpur
- tracing of footsteps of Lewis and Clark on a journey through American history
- learning to paint on Nantucket
- studying literature in London
- learning about coastal diversity on Cape Cod

You can also take Elderhostel e-courses much the same way you would with any distance learning institution. For example, they recently offered a course entitled "What life was like in the Roman Empire. " The cost of this course was $45.

The best way to explore this wonderful resource is to check our their web site at *www.elderhostel.org.* Or, you can call them at 1-877-426-8056 Monday through Friday from 9AM - 9PM.

Elderhostel is truly a venue of academic exploration where you learn by doing.

In co-operation with Elderhostel, the Close Up Foundation (*closeup.org/lifelong.htm*) offers five-night programs in our nation's capitol providing you with the opportunity to learn first hand about our government. These programs are actually learning vacations.

Take an Ivy League School Sponsored Educational Vacation

Here's an interesting educational alternative: Many top-ranked colleges and universities offer domestic and international study tours. The best part is that you do not have to be an alumnus. And, a faculty member usually leads tours.

The National Trust for Historic Preservation partners with many high-profile colleges to package educational tours (*nationaltrust.org/study_tours/*). A recent list of tours included adventure trips to The Galapagos Islands, and Tuscany, Italy.

The Schools offering these highbrow tours include Columbia, Harvard, Stanford and Yale.

Learn Something New While Having Fun: Take a Theme Cruise

Have you ever cruised before? If you have, you may have memories of a self-indulgent overeating orgy in which your fondest recollection is the five pounds you put on.

It seems as though cruise line companies are realizing that many baby boomers yearn for something more from cruising. They want to learn, and at the same time have some fun. Hence, the theme cruise has arrived as an enriching alternative to your standard cruise. Travel analysts say that this area is one of the few travel markets that are growing at a rate of about twenty percent a year.

So, you ask, what kinds of themes are available on cruises? There are probably as many themes as there are interests. You'll find a Macintosh workshop theme cruise for the Apple Computer enthusiast. Examples of other themes include fitness, jazz, film, cooking and antiquing.

Radisson Seven Seas (*raddison7seas.com*) has offered a twelve-day antique road show sailing from England to

Copenhagen featuring lectures and shopping at a cost of $7000 a person.

You can also travel with the Cunnard Line (*cunnard.com*) aboard the Queen Elizabeth Two and participate in themes such as classical music, British comedy, science fiction, and filmmaking.

The Maine Windjammer Association (*www.sailmainecoast.com*) out of Rockland Maine sails fourteen privately owned tall ships along the beautiful coast of Maine and focuses on themes from knitting to whale watching. A recent examination of rates indicated prices ranging from $400 to $800 per trip (more about this in Chapter 7).

The Delta Queen Steamboat Company (*deltaqueen.com*) provides theme cruises along the Mississippi River in paddle-wheel steamers offering programs on the Civil War with lectures and panel discussions by historians.

Crystal Cruises (*crystalcruises.com*) has been offering as many as thirty-three theme cruises per year. For example, they provide on-board state-of-the-art computer labs in their Computer University at Sea Program. Thirty complimentary courses are offered for their guests including e-mail, Word,

Excel, design, budgeting, web page design, and digital photo finishing.

Learn a New language In a Another Country

While we're on the subject of traveling to learn, here's a novel idea: Travel to another country to learn the native language.

In an effort to keep their economies stimulated, many governments of smaller countries are attempting to promote something relatively new called language tourism. Basically, you are immersed in the culture of the particular country while you study the language for an intensive period of time. People who participate in this type of instruction often experience the joy of learning about the country without feeling like a tourist. During the off hours, you can explore the topography of your surroundings.

Accommodations included with these programs vary. Normally you would stay with a host family or perhaps in an apartment. The duration will usually range from three weeks to about eight weeks depending on the package you select. You can elect to receive private instruction or be a part of a small group. You may expect a regimen of four or five hours of classes per day.

A popular destination for Spanish language instruction is Ecuador. The Canoa Spanish Language School (*ecuadorbeach.com/spanish_school*) features immersion instruction on a beautiful beachfront setting. Private teaching is scheduled at your convenience. Their four-week comprehensive program will cost you about $520 at the time of this writing. That price includes meals and accommodations. And, just think, you will be able to see the Galapagos or even trek to the nearby Andes Mountains in your free time.

The Ecuador Spanish Language School (*eduamazonas.com/*) offers a home stay approach in which the student lives with a family. They also teach through full Spanish immersion.

If you would like to learn a little of the Italian language, The Italian Language School (*scuolaleonardo.com*) offers two to four week sessions. Their schools are located in Rome, Florence, and Siena. The instruction is either private or small group. A two-week course starts at about $250 with host family or apartment accommodations available. The Italian Ministry of Education authorizes this school.

If you would like to explore this idea further, log onto your favorite search engine, type in the language instruction that your are interested in followed by the country and study the results. For example, a search for Spanish instruction would be typed as follows: "Spanish language instruction Costa Rica ". To make reasonably certain that you are enrolling in a quality program, it is probably better to look for some kind of state or provincial backing.

Alas, if you really are not the adventurous type, and would prefer to learn in a more domestic setting, there are simpler alternatives available to you. Certainly, various distance-learning courses offer language instruction, as do local adult education programs. There are wonderful software programs (such as the Rosetta Stone series) that will do the same thing.

CHAPTER 4: VOLUNTEERISM - GIVE SOMETHING BACK

The way I see it, if you are a professional retiree, or are in the contemplation stage, you've probably got many valuable life skill experiences behind you that you can share.

When I think about the spirit of volunteerism, I'm reminded of Jimmy and Rosalynn Carter and their long-term support for Habitat for Humanity International (*www.habitiat.org*). When the Carters left the Whitehouse rather unexpectedly, they were determined to continue their work in the community and fight for social justice. Their involvement with Habitat has led to homebuilding projects worldwide.

Speaking from my professional experience as a veteran teacher, there is nothing more rewarding than teaching another individual. This is especially meaningful when you have personal knowledge to share.

Edgar Bronfman, in his book *The Third Act* (G.P.Putnam's Sons, 2002), describes the process as "giving back." The subjects in his book indicated that volunteering expands horizons, bolsters personal growth, provides enormous self-satisfaction, increases your circle of acquaintances and support, and is just plain fun.

Do you enjoy working with people and look forward to helping others? Do you have the desire to keep on learning? If you answered yes to these questions, then it sounds to me as if you should be a volunteer.

The AARP has said that thirty-eight percent of Americans over sixty-five have expressed willingness to volunteer but simply don't know where to turn. Well folks, here are some suggestions:

Habitat For Humanity International
(*www.habitat.org*)

Habitat is a non-profit organization whose ultimate goals are the reduction of homelessness and the eradication of poverty types of housing. And, they have been tremendously successful.

Since their inception in 1975, Habitat has been able to house more than 625,000 people in 3000 communities both domestically and in other countries. The reality is that the homeowner participants become partners in the projects.

The construction and rehabilitation of the houses is accomplished through donations of labor, materials, and money.

The homeowners purchase the properties with mortgages that feature affordable no-interest loans. Further, the homes are sold on a no-profit basis. The deal is that the homeowners contribute their time in the construction and renovation of their homes as well as other, future projects. They may put in hundreds of hours of their own labor. Competent, well-trained people supervise all projects.

The selection of potential homeowners is need based, along with their commitment to Habitat as a partner.

If you are somewhat handy, or interested in being trained, log onto the Habitat website and click on the link that will search for the closest affiliate.

World Hunger Relief Inc. (*worldhungerrelief.org*)

Volunteers and professionals in this organization are deeply committed to ending world hunger by assisting those who need help with this basic need. Intensive training is provided in natural and sustainable farming techniques along with conserving and sharing resources.

More than three hundred interns in twenty countries have been trained in farming and re-forestation. Major projects have been undertaken in Haiti, Guatemala, and Kenya.

The organization is based in Waco, Texas. Volunteer openings are listed at the website.

Cross-Cultural Solutions (*crossculturalsolutions.org*)

This is a non-profit international volunteer organization that promotes cultural understanding. Volunteers work side by side with locals in the following countries: Brazil, China, Costa Rica, Ghana, Guatemala, India, Peru, Russia, Tanzania, and Thailand. One of the intended goals of for the volunteer is to gain a new perspective of the world and a renewed sense of personal growth. A fee is charged for participants, which goes toward the operation of the organization. Work includes teaching, daycare, and the creation of small business.

Literacy Volunteers (Local)

One of the most rewarding ways to volunteer is by becoming a literacy volunteer for a school system. Depending upon where you do this, the task may be as simple as reading a story to young school age children. Primary responsibilities might be to encourage enhancement of the students' reading skills. During my years as a teacher, these wonderful people served a variety of roles. Responsibilities included assisting in mathematics groups, acting as job coaches, and teaching life skills classes (banking, cooking, housekeeping). The New Haven Connecticut Public Schools has a program called the School Volunteers for New Haven, Inc. A goal for these volunteers is to improve the student's attitude towards school. Volunteers are recruited from retirees, professionals, trades people, business people and working people in general. Some of the responsibilities include mentoring younger at risk children. They also assist in arts, music, and science projects. Many even speak at career fairs. Some of these people are library assistants and classroom tutors.

Contact your local board of education to get the ball rolling. It is important to note here that no special skills are required. And, with all the emphasis these days on boosting standardized test scores, your help is needed more than ever.

Literacy Volunteers of America
(www.literacyvolunteers.org)

This agency provides literacy services to people who have severe needs. A major thrust here is to offer individuals opportunities to become independent, productive members of society. Local, state, and regional providers are fully networked. This affords greater opportunities for skill enhancement in the areas of reading, writing, English proficiency, problem solving and technology. In addition, instructional approaches are individualized to better serve students. Technology is used in an effort to make that learning more consistent.

Contact them through the website or call 1-315-422-9121.

Proliteracy Worldwide (*proliteracy.org*)

This is a literacy advocacy organization that addresses issues on a national level. They sponsor programs that help adults acquire important literacy skills. You can utilize drop down menus to find opportunities in your area.

International Executive Service Corps (*iesc.org*)

If you are a retired executive, you may be interested in sharing your knowledge with businesses in developing nations and in emerging democracies worldwide. By doing so you assist in the creation of a sustainable knowledge base, which encourages these firms to be more independent, and at the same time, you promote globalization. The Corps helps to strengthen non-government support organizations.

Services offered by IESC include managerial and technical assistance, market research studies, and access to financing and business planning.

SCORE - Service Corps of Retired Executives
(*www.score.org*)

Presently there are 10,500 retired and working professional volunteers in the SCORE network from around the world. They provide free business counseling and advice as a public service to all types of businesses, in all stages of development. Their responsibilities include virtual volunteering (more about this technique below) and e-mail counseling. Obviously, the use of a computer is a prerequisite for this organization.

VolunteerMatch (*volunteermatch.org*)

This is a nonprofit online service dedicated to finding you a great place to volunteer. Simply type in your zip code to find local volunteer opportunities matching your interests and schedule. The site features 31,000 organizations with 32,000 openings. As of this writing, they have made almost 2,000,000 referrals. This simple, effective service has already generated hundreds of thousands of volunteer referrals nationwide.

A relatively new component to VolunteerMatch is their link to Virtual Volunteering, a form of volunteerism that allows anyone to contribute their expertise without leaving home or office. More about this follows in the section below on Virtual Volunteering.

Servenet.org

A very complete list of volunteer organizations is presented. You can choose among organizations that most interest you. All you need to do is type in your zip code and search what is available in your area.

Big Brother/Big Sister (*www.bbbsa.org*)

Since it's founding in 1904, the major impetus of this organization has been youth mentoring. In 1977 both programs merged and their national headquarters was established in Philadelphia. Today, BBBSA concentrates on one-to-one mentoring relationships between adult volunteers and children. Most of the children in the program are from single parent families. At present, there are 500 programs around the country. In a study funded by the UPS, results indicated that sixty-four percent of the students developed more positive attitudes toward school, while fifty-eight percent achieved higher grades, and sixty percent noted improved relationships. Most parents of these children will agree that students do look forward to attending school. In fact, there are noticeably less unexcused absences and less of a chance of having to repeat a grade.

Most major cities house a Big Brother/Big Sister chapter. Make sure that you check out their wonderful website.

National Senior Service Corps (*www.seniorcorps.org*)

Over the last thirty years, the Corps has placed more that a half million volunteers in nationwide assignments through a network of projects. In order to participate in any of the Corps programs you must be at least fifty-five years of age. They really do try to individualize placements by utilizing the talents of older Americans.

The National Senior Service Corps controls three major programs:

1. The Foster Grandparent Program focuses their efforts on children with special or exceptional needs. This may include contributing support to children who are victims of abuse and neglect, tutoring children who have reading delays, counseling

troubled teenagers and young mothers, and helping children with more severe disabilities such as physical impairments.

Most foster grandparents serve about twenty hours per week, four hours a day, Monday through Friday. They must be sixty years of age or older and have a limited income. As of this writing they receive $2.65 per hour, which serves as a basic stipend. They also receive reimbursement for transportation, some meals during service, an annual physical examination, and insurance while on duty. In fiscal year 2001, over 30,000 Foster Grandparents tended to the needs of 275,000 young people.

I can tell you that these volunteers had an incredible impact on the self-esteem of the children that I taught. This was particularly evident where kids had little parental involvement in their lives.

2. The Senior Companion Program places volunteers with adults needing extra assistance in the community, such as a frail older person. The volunteer must be over the age of sixty and be able to volunteer twenty hours per week. As with Foster Grandparents, certain income restrictions apply. The hourly stipend is the same. The Senior Companion website, which is

linked through Seniorcorps, offers links to all of the state and local chapter.

3. The Retired and Senior Volunteer Program (RSVP) is one stop shopping for senior volunteers offering endless opportunities. Volunteers over fifty-five can be placed where their former career and life skills are needed. Flexible hours are featured.

The great thing about the Senior Corps is that it affords you opportunities to learn new skills. For example, some volunteers learn how to be effective tutors to young children. Some may organize community watch programs or environmental protection projects. Others may assist nonprofit organization boards with planning or resource development. The host agency provides all appropriate training.

Benefits of participating in the Senior Corps include helping your community, helping yourself, and receiving a small stipend.

To find out more information about the Corps, go to their website or call 1-800-424-8867.

Volunteer-in-Parks (National Park Service)

(*www.nps.gov/volunteer*)

The primary purpose of this program is to provide a vehicle through which the Park Service can accept and utilize voluntary help and services from the public. The Park Service attempts to find ways to meet the desires of the VIP while at the same time meeting its needs

Volunteers are accepted from the public without regard to race, creed, religion, age (a most significant consideration for us), sex, sexual orientation, national origin, or disability.

Park volunteers are very important to the NPS. Each year about 122,000 volunteers donate about 4,500,000 hours of service. They preserve and protect America's natural and cultural heritage for future generations.

Compensation for the types of service rendered varies. If you enjoy camping, you may be entitled to a free campsite. You may also receive free uniforms or residence. You may even receive a meal allowance. Some of the positions I looked into seem to offer a higher level of compensation for more extended periods of service.

Volunteer openings are clearly posted and described in detail on the NPS website. Examples of openings include interpreters, ambassadors, trail volunteers, guides, campground hosts, carpenters, tour guides, gardeners, visitor assistants, naturalists, and outreach volunteers. Available openings are posted at the appropriate National Park.

Depending on the position that is open, several weeks of training may be required. During that process, you learn much about the cultural history of the area you'll be working in, as well as the geology, ecology, and techniques for program preparation. You may even learn about public relations. It may be necessary to shadow a ranger or naturalist.

The campground hosts usually work four days per week, with their day beginning early. Their duties may involve trail clearing, dealing with entrance fee procedures, and keeping campsites presentable.

Most VIPs say that feel a great sense of satisfaction being able to return something to the National Park Service after many years of enjoying the parks. This service becomes even more meaningful in the face of decreasing resources and staff.

Since I've been camping in the National Park system for thirty-five years, I can personally attest to the dramatic difference those wonderful volunteers make in keeping our national treasures in beautiful condition. Here is a wonderful example of how you can make a meaningful contribution to an important resource.

Additional websites that will provide you with information on these positions are the Forest Service (*fs.fed.us* - click on "employment" and then "volunteers"), and the Bureau of Land Management (*www.blm.gov/*) Here are some specific examples of support services that VIPs provide:

- Yosemite National Park, California - Volunteers for the Astronomy Club at the park lead park visitors on stargazing events. Their generosity gives visitors a better understanding of the night sky.

- Mammoth Caves National Park, Kentucky - Each summer, forty volunteers participate in a cave restoration process in conjunction with the National Speleological Society. Their work includes renovation passageways and outdated lighting systems as well as cleaning cave formations and improving habitats for rare and endangered species.

- Everglades National Park, Florida - During the winter months volunteers at this park work at controlling invasive plant species throughout the park. This work has resulted in the restoration of diverse flora and fauna and has positively impacted the ecosystems in that area.

- Arches National Park, Utah - Volunteers here share their passion and knowledge for nature by leading visitors on walks throughout the hiking trails. They point out many of the park's details and pinpoint the spectacular views of canyons, mountains, and rivers.

Passport in Time Program (National Forest Service)(*passportintime.com*)(800-281-9176)

Here's a great opportunity for volunteers to make a significant difference in the preservation and restoration of historic sites around the country. The Passport in Time Program affords unique opportunities for people of all ages to work and learn alongside professional archaeologists and historians. It is, most definitely, a hands-on approach to preserving the nation's past. Many of the volunteers are RV'rs who combine their love of travel with a desire to help. Most projects last from two days to two weeks. Some last up to two months. College credits can be obtained in some cases. People with disabilities are encouraged to apply.

A fee PTT Traveler newsletter is published in March and September listing new projects with information (including duration, lodging and locations), reports, and photos of completed goals.

Accommodations vary widely according to the specific project. They can range from the most primitive camping to staying in motels (at the volunteer's expense). Many projects can accommodate RVs, often with hookups provided.

Prospective volunteers need to consider that they may face all types of weather conditions while participating in projects. Indeed, the PIT activities can be adventurous.

Examples of the nature of PIT projects include a 2000 documentation study of Ancient Pueblo people in Arizona's Kaibab National Forest, an excavation in Wyoming of an American Indian site, and a restoration of a turn-of-the-century log building in Black Hills National Forest in South Dakota. They have also excavated a silver mine in Missouri and unearthed a prehistoric stone cache in California.

U.S. Army Corps of Engineers Volunteer Clearinghouse (*www.lrn.usace.army.mil/volunteer*) (800-865-8337)

The Volunteer Clearinghouse attempts to match volunteers' needs and talents with the many projects the Corps undertakes. It cares for at least twelve million acres of land and water at four hundred sixty lakes across the United States. Most projects involve maintaining the recreation areas and protecting the natural resources.

Volunteer opportunities include trail building and maintenance, developing computer programs, photography, being a campground host, building wildlife habitats, working at the visitor centers, giving interpretive tours, presenting educational programs, and assisting in the development of archery ranges.

More than 70,000 volunteers have participated in the many projects that the Corps has undertaken.

If you log onto the Corps website, you can search state-by-state for available opportunities.

Peace Corps (*www.peacecorps.gov*)

When Lillian Carter, mother of the then president elect, joined the Peace Corps in 1966 at age sixty-eight, she was an aberration. The Peace Corps of that era was a youthful enterprise; only one percent of its volunteers were over fifty.

Times have certainly changed. Ten percent of the volunteers are over fifty. Many of the volunteers are retirees just like you seeking altruistic adventures.

Lauren Mitchell, the recruitment director of the Denver office, feels that older people make fantastic volunteers in that they offer a lot of expertise, maturity, and experience. Mitchell says, "They still think of it as being on your hands out in the fields. But now we do a lot of business advising, and teaching with computers." She feels that older volunteers are considered an invaluable asset. "Younger volunteers in the group really depend on them a lot for guidance," Mitchell says. "Many of today's senior volunteers had just started families when the Peace Corps began and did not have the opportunity to join," Mitchell said. "Now their kids are out of the house, they're healthy and financially stable. I couldn't do it then. Now I can."

Lillian Carter, who died in 1983, served as a Peace Corps nurse in India for two years. Her letters told of increasing joy in her work.

The Peace Corps is not alone in enjoying a surge of interest by older volunteers. Its domestic counterpart, AmeriCorps, hopes to expand senior programs that now encompass 500,000 volunteers.

Specific work assignments generally are made after a volunteer reaches the overseas country. Peace Corps leaders may generally divert older volunteers away from physically demanding tasks.

In many countries being an older person can have advantages. There is respect for age and reverence for maturity.

AmeriCorps/Vista (*www.americorps.gov*)

(1-800-942-2677)

Similar in nature to IESC, Americorps networks more than 2100 agencies involving more than 50,000 Americans yearly in service to these nonprofits. These volunteers help meet crucial needs in education, public safety, health, and the environment. Also included here are public and faith based agencies. Their youth programs revolve around teaching and mentoring, technology instruction, and the conducting of after school programs. Their environmental programs feature maintenance of parks and streams, and response to community disasters.

By the way, Americorps provides grants to Habitat For Humanity, the American Red Cross, and the Boys and Girls Clubs of America. Approximately three quarters of the AmeriCorps grant funding goes to State Commissions while the other quarter goes to national nonprofits that operate in more than one state.

AmeriCorps/Vista members have been helping to bring individuals and communities out of poverty for more than thirty-five years. The number of volunteers participating in their 1200 local programs was about 6000. If you log onto their website, you can view a list of current programs by state.

AmeriCorps*NCCC (National Civilian Community Corps) is a full time residential program for men and women between the ages of eighteen and twenty-four that lasts for a period of ten months. The types of projects volunteers participate in include public health and safety and disaster relief.

Americorps members serve in teams of ten to fifteen. Be reminded that if you are interested in becoming a member you'll be asked to commit to a ten to twelve month period of service either full or part time. Full time members are eligible to receive stipend awards to pay for college, graduate school, or to pay back college loans. You can also receive an annual living allowance.

Global Volunteers (*www.globalvolunteers.org*) (1-800-487-10740)

Global Volunteers sends teams to work on community projects in nineteen nations year-round. No special skills are necessary. Tax-deductible service program fees cover food, lodging, ground transportation, and project expenses. Airfare is not included. The following examples represent some of the recent projects.

> * A two-week project in Costa Rica was completed which involved the renovation and organization of a high school public library. The group included students, a lawyer, a computer engineer and several teachers. They worked shoulder to shoulder with local adults and high school students. During their free time they hiked, swam, toured the forests, and visited an active volcano.
> * Volunteers were needed to teach English at a summer camp in Crete. The students, who rarely had a chance to

practice speaking English, were from several local villages. Informal classes consisted of crafts, songs and games.

* Workers on a Blackfoot Reservation in Browning, Montana, installed playground equipment, repaired rooms, provided computer training and worked with youths at a detention center.

Shriners (*www.shrinershq.org*) (800-237-5055)

The Shrines support many philanthropic causes. In 1920 they formed the Shriners Hospital for crippled children. Soon after they built twenty-two other orthopedic children hospitals around the country to support such problems or injuries as clubfoot, scoliosis, and cerebral palsy. In 1962 they expanded their services to include children suffering from severe burns. To date, the organization has helped more than 650,000 children. One of the key features of these hospitals is that all the care and rehabilitation is provided totally without charge to any patient under the age of eighteen. Most of their money comes from donations or fund raising. This is a great organization to belong to if you are a member of the Good Sam Club and you have an RV. Many members travel around the country to the various events. The Shriners are looking for volunteers with expertise in all areas.

Heifer International (*heifer.org*) (800-422-0474)

In the 1930's, while a civil war raged in Spain, Dan West, a mid-western farmer, decided to help families there by giving out milk to hungry children. He felt that what was needed was a cow more than a cup of milk. In this fashion hungry families could continue to feed themselves through a sustainable lifestyle. In return, they could help another family become self-reliant by passing on to them one of their gift animal's female calves.

Heifer animals offer hungry families around the world a way to feed themselves and become more self-reliant. Children receive nutritious milk or eggs, and communities go beyond meeting immediate needs to fulfilling dreams. Farmers also learn sound agricultural techniques.

This idea has caught on to the point that families in 115 countries have enjoyed better health, more income and the joy of helping others.

Heifer maintains regional centers around the country that can provide you with educational resources and materials. They can also answer your questions about volunteering, study tours, and ways to involve your church or community organization. Call the toll free number to find the closest regional office.

Volunteers play an integral role in Heifer's effort to alleviate poverty and hunger and promote nutrition and well-being.
You can volunteer at the following:

- One of three Heifer learning centers at the following locations: Heifer Ranch, Perryville, Arkansas; Overlook Farm, Rutland, Massachusetts; Ceres Center, Ceres, California
- One of Heifer's Regional Centers
- Speaking at a church of community group or company
- International Volunteer Opportunities - concentrating on helping families around the world in need with a fresh start
- Study Tours - travel and learn by visiting a Heifer project worldwide

Other volunteer opportunities include participating in one of the following:

- Community Representatives - A volunteer from a geographical area will address any person or group (including schools) that would like to know more about Heifer.

- Media Volunteers - Writers may be needed for the media.

- Organizational Representative - These volunteers represent Heifer in a specific group such as a church, the Lions, Kiwanis, or Rotary Club even a 4-H Club.

There are many opportunities for full-time volunteers at the Learning Centers. Full-timers go for a week to a year and receive housing and a monthly stipend.

Here's an example of a Heifer success story:

In drought ravaged eastern Guatemala, women and girls are responsible for gathering enough water for their families and animals. This involves many trips to the nearest source while balancing twenty-pound jugs on their heads. In an effort to ease this laborious chore, Heifer has been sending goats and volunteers to the area. A goat may only drink one gallon of water per day as opposed to a single cow that would consume eighteen gallons. Further, goats are better adapted to the rocky highlands of the area and eat less food. As a result of this effort, the children are spending more time in school and the number of children quitting school has been reduced.

My wife and I have begun volunteering for Heifer. We have been doing presentations at various schools to promote their "Read to Feed" (*readtofeed.org*) program. Students actually see that they are changing the world in a positive way. They read a variety of books and follow a specific curriculum. Literacy skills are enhanced by the activities. Fundraising goals are set and sponsors pledge money based on the amount of books that these students read. Finally, they decide which animals to symbolically purchase for struggling families.

For more details about Heifer go to the website.

Farm Sanctuary (*farmsanctuary.org*) (607-583-2041)

If you love animals and have a passion for animal rights, you may be interested in Farm Sanctuary. A major goal is the protection and rescue of farms animals. They operate a coast-to-coast network of shelters that specialize in adoption. They seek to educate millions of people like you, about farm animal suffering. They've actually been able to enact legislation regarding farm animal practices. Volunteer opportunities include participating in various farm chores or helping out with administrative tasks.

AARP Driver Safety Program (*aarp.org/life/drive/*) (888-227-7669)

In Chapter 1 of this book I suggested that you might be interested in sharpening your driving skills through the AARP Driver Safety Program. Well, they could surely use your services as a volunteer in this program. In fact, the program could not readily exist without its volunteers.

AARP provides its volunteers reimbursement for facilitating courses as well as a thorough orientation and training program. Openings include Coordinator positions as well as instructors.

Participants in this program gain a strong sense of satisfaction knowing that they have contributed to the health, safety, and happiness of others in their community.

Virtual Volunteering

If you enjoy working on your computer and really have it in your heart to be a volunteer, why not do it virtually.

Basically speaking, this type of volunteer service takes place on the Internet. And, it comes in many forms. Agencies really do benefit from virtual volunteering as it encourages expansion of their programs by allowing for more volunteer participation and the creation of new areas to work in.

If you are physically incapacitated, have transportation issues, or have time constraints, this venue may open up a whole new world of volunteering opportunities for you. In addition, you can even virtually volunteer at your place of work. Of course, you'll need to be somewhat proficient with your computer in order to be successful here.

Serviceleader.org is a great site to explore and learn about virtual volunteering resources. Past online assignments include various research projects, newsletter editing, graphic design, researching elected officials, translation, and proofreading. Examples of categories of volunteers are as follows:

Technical assistance participants do task based assignments (research, consulting, proofreading, translation) while direct contact volunteers have contact with the client or service rep (mentoring, language instruction). An informal volunteer simply supplies informal support without training.

Another terrific opportunity for virtual volunteering is Elder Wisdom Circle (*elderwisdomcircle.org*). Basically, the goal here is to share the infinite elder knowledge and wisdom its volunteers have accumulated. That said, an interested party could seek advice on any topic. Responses are offered through e-mail.

The only criteria you must meet to join the Wisdom Circle, is that you must be at least sixty years of age. If you check out the website, it becomes immediately apparent that people of all backgrounds and levels of education participate as volunteers.

As previously indicated, VolunteerMatch (*volunteermatch.org*) offers a large number of links for virtual volunteering. Simply click on a link and you will be presented with a description and contact information to any of the hundreds of postings. Some of the many categories include health and medicine, sports and recreation, disabled, women, religion, computers, and children and youth.

CHAPTER 5: HOBBIES

The dictionary defines a hobby as a "spare time activity". If you interpret that meaning broadly, almost anything you do in your leisure time can be a hobby. Just think of all the different things that you do during the course of your day beyond working. For many people, unfortunately, things like eating, sleeping, and watching television may be the first things that come to mind. It just may be that after all of those years of working long, hard hours, you simply do not have any other interests. Your routine may have been steadfast, leaving little room for change. This, my friends, is one of the greatest reasons why people dread retirement.

Hopefully, after you've pondered the information in this chapter, new and more creative ideas will come to mind and your perspective on retirement will be recharged. The following paragraphs contain examples of popular hobbies that you might consider trying. Remember: Be bold and adventurous! You are attempting to find the new you.

Make certain that you've reviewed the suggestions I made in Chapter 2 for physical activities, especially if you live in a climate that is conducive to outdoor recreation.

Fun With Technology

Now it's time for a discussion on how you can learn to be a technology wizard. As you know by now, this is an area that it is dear to me since I did spend many years as technology specialist. In this role I taught many adults and students how to become proficient and have fun.

In order for this to make sense, I'm going to make certain assumptions.

First, I'll presume that you have little or no experience with computers and the digital wizardry that goes with them. If, in fact, you are more advanced, then go through this section quickly.

Second, since I'm not writing an instructional manual, I will select which goals you might be interested in. I will start with that subject first.

As indicated previously, I recently took an extended trip around the country that lasted several months. During this trip, I observed the common uses that retirees make of technology. Since you are in the retirement stage the following discussion will be based on pleasurable uses.

You will most likely use technology for the following reasons:

1. E-mail (especially your grandchildren)

2. Surfing the Internet for fun

3. Digital photography, and movie editing

4. Shopping

5. Word processing

6. Other hobbies (cooking, art,)

7.Banking

8.Investing

If you have absolutely no experience with a computer, I suggest that you take a basic course. Even if you have some skills, additional advanced training can never hurt, especially with the developing pace of digital and wireless technology.

An easy way to begin the process is to check with the town or city within which you reside, to see what is available through programs such as adult education. There, the course offerings usually include development of beginner to advance level skills with training in both hardware and software.

Check with your local college or university including community colleges. If you are a senior citizen (age sixty and beyond) you may be eligible to take a free or reduced tuition course. If these alternatives are not available, you may be able to obtain the services of a technology trainer. These people either come to your home or you go to their office. If you have the financial ability to do this, you'll get all the attention you need. Or, if have a friend or family member that can train you, that is even better. This technique usually works well as the environment for learning is more relaxed.

You can purchase instructional aids from your local bookstore that are very easy to understand. Also, your local computer retailer should be able to assist you, especially if you purchase a home setup component with your PC. Many of these retailers offer their own classes on premises. I've also found that most literature that accompanies new computers is very self explanatory and easy to understand. Those tutorials are step-by-step with diagrams.

Computer training is also offered online. These programs allow you to work at your own pace. Services are offered privately as well as through distance learning programs as described in this chapter and Chapter 3.

Gateway Computer Company (*gateway.com/training*) offers computer training via a CD tutorial, or online. The training is taught beginning with an emphasis on the basics, followed by instruction on multimedia applications, concluding with lessons on the Internet. Online subscriptions are only ninety-nine dollars per year (ten percent off for AARP members) and are accessible twenty-four hours per week seven days a year. You can also sign up for a sixth month subscription for thirty dollars. The good thing here is that you can work for as little or as long as you desire.

AARP (*aarp.org/learntech/computers/*) offers a series of free computer tutorials. In fact, you don't even have to be a member to take advantage of this instruction. There are a wide variety of "how to" technology links offered. The basic Internet tutorial is quite thorough with a graduated approach leading to more advanced Internet browsing.

You can also check out CyberSeniors (*cyberseniors.org*)(1-800-676-6622). Elizabeth Isele has trained more than 15,000 seniors in her not-for-profit organization during the past few years. Her students are taught to navigate the web with an emphasis on utilizing online resources. Seniors conduct most of the workshops, which complements her philosophy of encouraging seniors to learn from one another.

The community college system of Connecticut offers master computer training online (*gwcc.howtomaster.com*) with around the clock access. Two hundred forty courses are available including most Microsoft software, digital imaging, using a palm organizer, and business writing. Their fees begin at only fifty-eight dollars.

However you do it, it is most important that you learn the basics before you move on. You must become proficient in the following procedures:

- Use of the mouse (most important)
- Use of the keyboard
- Use of peripherals
- Putting in and ejecting a CD or DVD
- Entering and exiting programs
- Basic core operations
- Understanding the different drives and their functions

Once you learn the basic skills, it is very important that you practice. If you do not currently own a computer, one suggestion is to go to your local library and play. Most libraries offer free high speed Internet access.

And then, of course, as you become more comfortable with all of this, it's easy to progress to more fun things described here such as multimedia editing, making CDs, and even making your own DVDS from still pictures or movies.

Some years ago, when I was still working in the public school system, a new principal arrived on the scene. She had absolutely no idea how to use a computer. The year was 1999. Her first instruction to me was to teach her the basics. At the time, she had a great deal of difficulty using the mouse. The hand eye coordination can be very challenging in this endeavor. With a little practice, and a short tutorial from the computer, and me, she took off. She has become very proficient.

Once you've had a bit of experience with the computer, and you discover what a joy it is, it may the right moment to consider purchasing one. The only way you can feel comfortable with the tools of technology is to play around with them. A basic system that costs under $1000 should do the trick. Certainly you'll need to get at least 256mb of ram (memory), and a large enough hard drive to store lots of pictures or music that you may download. Additionally, with the increasing popularity of high-speed wireless technology, you may want to consider buying a wireless card. This feature will allow you to go online with no wires. If you travel with your computer, this is particularly useful.

E-mail is one of the greatest social inventions of our time. You can keep in contact with people all over the world. And, you can do this from your home, car, or anywhere you are on vacation. If you are somewhat shy about using the phone, this method of communication is for you. As you become more proficient, you can join a chat room where you can actually converse with other people online. So you see, you really do not need to talk with other people face to face!

With today's digital technology, it's easier than ever to send e-mail with attachments of pictures or movies that you've taken. You can purchase a simple inexpensive digital still camera, or movie camera, and hook it up to your computer and you are in business. There are many types of photo software available to you so you can edit, copy, and organize your stills and movies. You can even make photo albums, greeting cards, a video CD, and lots more.

The Internet serves many purposes for the surfer. Many people do the bulk of their shopping that way. Most department stores offer very complete websites. And, you can often find better deals online due to the lower overhead of these online companies. It is also easy to make your travel arrangements the same way with airlines offering substantial discounts. Make sure that you check the travel links in the Website Directory of this book. I've listed the most popular online companies.

As you already realize, the Internet puts the world at your fingertips. Here are some additional examples of what you can do:

- Visit museums

- Travel to foreign countries (virtually)

- Visit with friends and relatives while online

- Take courses (as described in Chapter 3)

- Buy an automobile

- Download music

- Learn just about anything that you are interested in.

In most cases it's just a matter of doing a search to point you in the right direction. If you do an online search, you'll recall that I advised you to use Google, as it is a very highly rated search engine. Be as specific and brief as possible when typing in the wording.

Another very popular use that retirees find for their computers is word processing. In addition to writing e-mail, writing letters and writing a book or poems are just some other creative uses. If you go a step further, learning how to use a database will allow you to sctup a budget and basically chart anything that requires numbers. The most popular word processing programs (Word, Works, Appleworks) offer splendid tutorials, which will get you going immediately. Just think; you'll be able to make posters, write newsletters, make graphs, and even catalog your books.

If you need to brush up (or learn) your keyboarding skills there are many wonderful typing tutors for sale. I recommend the newest version of the Mavis Beacon program. You'll need to practice the lessons on a regular basis. When I taught myself to keyboard, part of my daily routine was to practice about thirty minutes per day. You can also do this through your local adult education program.

After speaking with many currently retired people, I have discovered an all too common attitude that many retirees possess. They feel that they are too old to learn a new skill. My answer to that is "humbug". It is really very easy to learn the technology these days (especially with all the great accompanying tutorials). But you do need to practice your newly learned skills. Remember, we decided early in this book that you are going to reinvent yourself. In order to do that, you must try some of the ideas that I have put forth.

Learn to be an artist

Have you ever wondered if you possess artistic talent? Maybe you've doodled on a napkin or two and aroused your curiosity. Have you ever worked on one of those paint by number kits and realized that you really enjoyed doing it. You may never realize your potential until you try to develop those talents.

My ninety-year-old mother in law began to paint in her seventies. She attended art classes at local universities that she audited, and enrolled in classes at a local art school. She also attended classes at local community programs at her town recreation center. Much of her work has been featured in area shows.

If you are interested in pursuing your artistic talents, get involved with the local art guild in your area. They are a great resource for instruction and exhibition of your work. The personal input by the other members may turn out to be an important learning tool for you. Also, make certain that you visit art museums and galleries either in person or online. Many art galleries offer instructional classes. Making these visitations will surely be a great source of inspiration for you.

One of the most famous museums within which you can do a virtual tour of is Le Louvre, in Paris, France (*www.louvre.fr*). The Harvard University Art Museum site (*www.artmuseums.harvard.edu*) offers interactive online exhibits and collections. The fantastic Art Museum Network (*amn.org*) presents links to the world's leading art galleries with over 200 members. They also offer news links as well as an excellent search mechanism. The Virtual Library Museum (*vlmp.museophile.com*) provides a directory of worldwide online museums.

And, of course, do not forget to explore your local adult education and community recreation programs for additional course offerings. A recent check of some adult education course offerings in the northeast indicates classes in drawing, pastels, and oils.

Here are some other unique suggestions:

Correspondence Schools

Yes, they still do exist. A word of caution, however, is warranted. Some experts view this type of study strictly as a hobby. This is fine if that is your intended purpose. In their view, serious artists study in a studio setting at a school. It is their opinion it is difficult to learn proper technique without being in the presence of an instructor. Of course, this is a matter of opinion.

Proponents of correspondence courses advocate advantages such as emphasis on important basics including composition, design and tonal values. Students receive textbooks that illustrate each step in the process of drawing and painting, and sometimes are even given supplies to complete assignments. Programs attempt to provide what is taught in a regular art class. The approach here is that students learn by doing, not by teacher feedback. Many instructors at art schools are overloaded with students. Teacher responses may be brief or even generic.

The following is a list of resources for those of you interested in correspondence schools:

- General information - Distance Education and Training Council, (202) 234-5100 (*detc.org*) - for questions on the legitimacy of correspondence schools

- Art Instruction Schools - (612) 362-05060 (*www.artists-ais.com*)

- Gordon School of Art - (800) 210-1220 (*www.newmasters.com*)

Online Coursework

Many experts agree that this type of education is different from correspondence education. Most of the coursework is offered by degree granting institutions and taught by the same faculty members who teach at those institutions. Students communicate with each other through e-mail. Most of the time, work is posted on the Internet. This permits everyone in the class to see it, and if necessary, critique it.

Lessons are posted on the web. Instructors make assignments with specific due dates. Students may photograph their work and transmit it to the online classroom (it's really not difficult). Grades are based on the quality of the student's participation and work.

The following is a list of resources for those of you interested in online art instruction:

- Art Institute Online - (877) 872-8869 (*aionline.edu*)

- Maryland Institute College of Art - (410) 669-9200 (*www.mica.edu*)

- Minneapolis College of Art and Design (800) 874-6223

- Parsons School of Design (212) 229-5880 (*parsons.edu*)

Gardening

For many years, as part of my profession, I ran a greenhouse and a garden program for my students. I cannot stress enough how wonderfully relaxing and stimulating this activity is. It is indeed, quite therapeutic, especially when the fruits of your labor present themselves.

Basically speaking, if you have a few sunny spots in your house, as well a spot for a garden, you can participate in this delightfully rewarding hobby at any time during the year. You may reside in a community that has plots available to the public in a community garden. The cost of these seasonal rentals is usually quite reasonable. If you know a bit about gardening, these community plots are a blessing since they usually provide you with good quality soil and an easily accessible water supply.

There are many gardeners out there that enjoy working with specialized collections including orchids and African violets. If you have an interest in this the public library is a good place to start as well as your local florist.

Hopefully, by now you have a home computer. (I assume that if I keep reminding you about this, you will finally get one.) Don't forget to look at the great gardening websites listed in the

Website Directory at the end of this book. At the *garden.org* site sponsored by the National Gardening Association, you'll find answers to most of your questions. This is also a great place to go if you are a beginning gardener. The *gardenguides.com* site is very well organized and features tip sheets and more than 170 links. The Garden Helper (*www.thegardenhelper.com*) is especially helpful to beginners with their houseplants. The advice here is from garden guru Bill Beaurain. And, of course, look at the Better Homes and Gardens website (*www.bhg.com*) with A-Z advice on landscaping and houseplants.

If you need more gardening advice, and you have cable TV (and who doesn't), watch the House and Garden Network (HGTV) for timely tips. And, be certain to check with your local garden center. I've seen many local advertisements for workshops given by these establishments.

Needless to say, your local library is a great resource for you. Also, you'll find that local adult education and park recreation programs offer a variety of horticultural course offerings.

Sing or play a musical instrument

When I was much younger, I played the clarinet, saxophone, and flute. I can clearly remember how much I enjoyed both the challenge and the music, and how good I was at playing those instruments.

Those fond memories led me to believe that this may be a fun thing to resume. I also concluded that this is one of those activities that will keep my mental acuity on track. So, my wife picked up a used clarinet for me at a tag sale and I began playing again after at least a thirty-year hiatus.

Much to my delight, I really do enjoy playing again. I've re-taught myself lost skills and am making remarkable progress. In fact, as of this point in time, I'm actually quite far along in a Mozart Clarinet Concerto. I simply bought some method books and have begun practicing on a regular basis. Thus far, I have not taken any lessons. Furthermore, since my wife is a pianist, we've decided to perform some duet pieces on a volunteer basis at assisted living centers, senior centers, and hospitals. The reality is that we are giving back by volunteering, and at the same time enjoying a fulfilling hobby.

So, if I can relearn these skills so can you. If you enjoy singing, join a community chorus. If you currently play an instrument, join a community band. You can also look into singing in a church or synagogue choir. How about taking private music lessons? Many towns and cities offer lessons and group experiences as part of their adult education programs. In addition, they may even offer enrichment programs that will enhance your understanding of the various forms of music.

Cooking

Many people find that the art of cooking is beyond their capabilities or interest level. If you find that cooking is a chore, then you may not be interested in furthering your skills. However, if you perceive culinary endeavors to be a true art form (or at least fun), then you can improve upon your talents by going to the nearest bookstore or library. There you can pick up instructional materials. My home cooking library is probably as good as any bookstore. Most of our books were obtained by my wife at tag sales, flea markets, and sale racks at bookstores.

Your greatest resource for this particular hobby is probably the Internet. All you need to do is a search on Google (*google.com*) (highest rated search engine by PC Magazine) and type in the specific topic you are interested in. For example, try typing in "tilapia" for some delectable fish recipes. Two wonderful online resources are foodtv (*foodtv.com*) and meals.com (*www.meals.com*). Both of these sites include wonderful step-by-step suggestions from the famous chefs. Make sure that you also check out the *cooking.com* site. This site features cooking accessories, recipes, menus, and cooking tips from well-known chefs.

Again, do not forget classes that you may be able to take as part of your local adult education programs.

Here is an example of a really cool way to expand upon your passion for cooking: Consider taking a study stint at a culinary institute. For example, the Culinary Institute of America (*ciachef.edu*) offers various five-day programs at both of their campuses. They are located in Hyde Park, New York and St. Helena, California. Some of these programs are geared towards techniques, skills and presentation of personal cooking and baking in the home. You can learn to grill, braise, deep fry and so forth. So, if you have thought about cooking like the pros, you may want to spend a week in this kind of unique program.

As a person relatively new to the world of cooking, I've found that two of the most rewarding and relaxing things to make are bread and homemade pasta. With proper tools and techniques you too will be appreciative of all the praise you'll receive. I recently learned how to make sushi, which my family and I all crave. Learning this technique was indeed very gratifying.

Antique Collecting

If you are interested in antiques, I'm sure that you realize how important it is that you know what you're doing. That would include knowledge of materials and value. Obviously, you do not want to be taken advantage of by an unscrupulous dealer. There are many resources out there for you to take advantage of.

A good book to start with is *The Unofficial Guide to Collecting Antiques,* by Sonia Weiss (IDG Books Worldwide). You'll learn important bits of antique wisdom including where to look, how to find the best prices, when to sell, tips on foolproof appraisals, and advice on seeing through fakes.

I also suggest that you visit your local library. *Amazon.com* sells a wide variety of books on specific antiques such as wine, trunks and their restoration, and gold.

A good website to visit is *antiqueresources.com.* There is a wide variety of discussion forums and even a link to the Antique Doctor who features a discussion of timely issues and an "ask the doctor" a question format. You can even learn how to setup an online antique mall. There's also a classified section available as well as auction and book information. You can actually take a virtual tour of some items, get an appraisal, and purchase online.

Antiqueweb.com features seventy-five links to information on all sorts of antiques such as autos, clocks, art, and comics.

Visit local attractions

My wife and I discovered, soon after we retired, that we had rarely ever visited many of the noted local New England attractions. As we live near the Yale Community, many opportunities availed us. For example, we began to explore the many museums, became subscribers to their local theater, and attended some of the local concerts.

I suggest that you become familiar with your town or city website as well as your state website. Most government sites have tourist attraction links that you can click on that will readily familiarize you with wonderful places to visit in your area. Admission prices are usually posted and a guided tour available online. Don't forget to use any qualifying discounts you may be entitled to such as AAA (*aaa.com*) or AARP (*aarp.org*).

Make sure that you check with local Chamber of Commerce since they often carry information about local attractions.

If you know the whereabouts of tourism kiosk in your area, an abundance of information awaits you. In many states these kiosks are located on a major highway. There you'll find guidebooks, maps, and brochures galore. I must admit that I would have missed quite a bit had I not visited these stops on my trip around the country.

The following are some examples of places to visit that are typically found in many locations:

-Seaports

-Castles

-Historic parks

-Art museums

-Amusement parks

-Historic houses

-Observatories

-Famous gardens

-Other historic sites

-Sports arenas and parks

-State parks

-Automobile racetracks

Collections

If you are the type of person that prefers simple, stationary hobbies, then putting together a collection is for you. Basically speaking, anything goes. Most common collections are easy to begin. Hobby stores can supply you with starter kits to get you going with stamps and coins. If you need advice as to how to begin, there are many chat rooms on the Internet to assist you. Look into subscribing to *Hobbyist Magazine*.

As you can imagine, collections can become very complicated and expensive depending upon where your interests lie. I have a friend who traveled all over the place to collect garden tractors. That same person recently switched over to Nash Metropolitan automobiles. He indicated to me that a great Internet source that has been very helpful to him is Ebay (ebay.com). You can find just about anything to bid on there.

Other examples of popular collectibles include action figures, antiques, books, comics, dolls, miniatures, model cars, and remote control vehicles.

Renovations and home repair projects

This next section is most relevant to you if you own property or you have the desire to become more of a handy person perhaps with the intention of helping others (friends or family). May I suggest the Habitat for Humanity (*www.habitat.org*) if you are able to give of your time?

When I retired, I began a series of long overdue projects around the house. At this point in my life, it was a good feeling to know that I now had the time for these things and that I could take my time. This extra time allowed me to learn how to improve my skills. So, I began studying reference books, taking courses, and researching the specific projects that I wanted to complete on the Internet. I've found that the best way to improve your handyperson skills is by actually doing the work.

One of the things we wanted to do was to develop more sophisticated home decorating skills. My wife was interested in learning how to faut paint. So, we first visited a home improvement store, which happened to be Lowe's. For your information, the sales staff at most of these places is very knowledgeable and helpful. They have available a variety of publications and videos to assist you in your work. We also learned in greater detail the process of removing vinyl wallpaper and a variety of other techniques.

If you have a specific task to complete by all means log on to the Internet and go to *google.com*. Type in the name of the project and great advice will appear from a variety of expert sources. Make sure that you bookmark some of the better websites for future reference in case you need further assistance in other areas. A most important consideration here is that you learn by doing. Pick up some scrap materials at the local lumberyard to practice with. You'll find it quite helpful to log onto the Do It Yourself Network (*diynet.com*). The site features a plethora of links and tips relating to home improvement, including woodworking, kitchen renovations, and decorating. There's an abundance of tutorials, message boards, and planning tools.

Remember that all-important resource for learning these skills: your local adult education program. In addition, I've noticed that some community colleges offer programs that will teach you some of these basic skills.

Investing

There are many investing resources to assist you. The most current information is usually available on the Internet (check out some of the site suggestions in the Web Site Directory of this book), or through frequently published financial newspapers. With the state of the rapidly changing financial markets, you'll need to keep up with the most current data available.

An investment club is a great way for novice investors to pool their knowledge and learn about the market together. Normally, funds are pooled and club members invest together. Each member pays monthly dues. These dues go into the investment fund. Major advantages of being part of a club like this include the knowledge you can gain about the stock market as well as improving money management skills. If you are interested in forming an investment club, the National Association of Investors Corporation (NAIC) can assist you. You can call them at 248-583-6242 or go to their website at *www.better-investing.org.* They can provide you with bylaws, partnership guidelines, and a variety of online investment tools. Their philosophy is that if you work hard enough you can make money in the stock market. Another useful site on investment clubs is the Motley Fool (*fool.com/investmentclub*). Women can find help at Chicks Laying Nest Eggs (*chickslayingnesteggs.com*)

Or, you can simply form an investors group that meets on a regular basis to discuss various types of investments. This is more of an informal get together.

Some of the bigger investment firms such as Fidelity (*fidelity.com*) or Vanguard (*vanguard.com*) provide very timely advice at no charge. They offer information and calculators that can help with retirement issues, college funding planning, and general tax implications. They also keep you abreast of current market conditions and trends.

Many of the financial magazines and newspapers offer timely advice as well. *Smartmoney* (*www.smartmoney.com*) and *Morningstar* (*morningstar.com*) are two that come to mind. Some of these companies will provide you with limited information and then ask you to join with an annual fee. In my opinion, it can be better to subscribe to the online versions of these publications as opposed to subscribing to the printed version since the online versions may be updated more frequently. *Money Magazine* may be more suited towards long-term action since it is printed far in advance of publication. Of course a highly reliable and respected financial newspaper is the Wall Street Journal.

Model building

When you were a kid, remember the model kits that you saw in the hobby store. You could build models of just about anything. Years ago, this hobby was very popular. You could buy model kits at a variety of stores. Now, most of the availability is at hobby stores.

Handcrafts

If you are lucky enough to have a handcraft center near you, you'll be able to take classes in many of the following crafts:

Pottery making

Weaving

Basket making

Watercolors

Acrylic design

Oil painting

Sculpture

Genealogy

Have you ever had the desire to start a family tree? Do you think you may want to learn more about your ancestors? As you can probably imagine, there are a great variety of resources available. You can start by going to the public library. Or, you can go online.

On the web, log onto *www.genealogy.com.* This is PC Magazine's Editors choice for the best genealogy site. It's easy to start your family tree here with step-by-step guidance. You can also try *www.genhomepage.com.* This site is chock full of genealogy links that will provide you with abundant resources. There's also Jewish Genealogy *(www.jewishgen.org)* that boasts being the home of Jewish genealogy. Finally, Roots Web (*genealogy.org*) offers a free search mechanism, which will easily begin the process.

Learn or Pursue a Hobby: A Vacation Challenge

Here's a great idea! Why not take a vacation that will teach or enhance your skills for a hobby that you have an interest in.

Ghost Ranch (*ghostranch.org*) is situated on 21,000 idyllic acres of land in Abiquiu, New Mexico. These surroundings serve as source of inspiration for all of those who enroll in the art and culture courses offered. The ranch is owned and operated by the Presbyterian Church as an educational program and retreat. Some of their courses are offered in conjunction with Elderhostel.

Here's a partial list of some of the course offerings:

Blacksmithing

Quilting

Woodcarving

Pottery

Spanish tinwork

Fabric landscaping

Scrapbook making

Archaeology

Meditation

Opera and music

The average cost per week ranges from $500 - $900 including housing.

Folkschool.org offers 450 courses in the Appalachian mountains of North Carolina. Their curriculum includes music, photography, blacksmithing and woodcarving. You can take a course in dulcimer making. The cost is $600 - $750 per week.

If you have musical talent, check out *hiddenvalleymusic.org* in Carmel Valley, California. Their focus is on choral, big band, and orchestral performances on all levels. They offer programs forty-two weeks per year. The classes rigorously prepare the participants for a performance at week's end. The emphasis here is on the process of working together. Costs range from $495-$625 per week.

CHAPTER 6: CULTURAL INTERESTS

Hopefully, when you retire (or if you are retired), you won't become a couch potato. I know lots of people who have become professionals in that area. It's easy to see why gradual decay has begun setting in.

The cultural arts present a splendid way for you to become personally enriched through a variety of mediums. There are so many wonderful artists out there (writers, authors, playwrights and composers) that have so much to say. And, you are provided with yet another opportunity to keep the brain cells active.

If you are interested in participating in the arts, the latest research does indicate that the arts can keep you healthy.

Dr. Gene D. Cohen of George Washington University's Center on Aging, Health, and Humanities studied three hundred men and women participating in several arts programs around the country. These programs included The Seniors Singers Chorale, an Arlington Virginia based chorus (*levineschool.org*), The National Center for Creative Aging in Brooklyn (718-398-3870), and the Center for Elders and Youth in the Arts in San Francisco (*gioa.org/programs/art/art.html*). Early findings indicate that arts participants schedule fewer doctor appointments, have fewer incidents of depression, have higher morale, and more involvement in outside activities.

Theater

Most towns and cities offer an abundance of theatre offerings for your delight. If you are interested, you can subscribe for the season at discounted rates. You may even have the chance to attend matinee performances so that you do not have to go out in the evenings. If you live near an urban area, as we do, you may even be able choose the types of theater you wish to attend. We subscribe to a variety of theater that feature drama, comedies, and musicals.

If you don't live in area that features theater, perhaps you can travel to a city to see a show. There are a variety of Internet sites to help you make your plans. In fact, the whole process can be both fun and a learning experience for you, particularly if you are new to computer use.

For example, if I want to see a Broadway show, I log onto *broadway.com* for schedules and great deals on tickets. I then proceed to the Metro North website (*metronorth.com*) to check the train schedules. Then, of course, I have to check the weather for the day at The Weather Channel (*weather.com*). If I choose to make a day of it and have dinner, there are a variety of websites that feature restaurants and their menus along with prices. I log onto Google and type in "New York City restaurants."

You may be able to participate in day trips sponsored by the local senior center or recreation department. My research has shown that the cost of these trips is generally very reasonable as these organizations are non-profit.

You may find that the cost difference of taking a trip with the aforementioned groups is negligible compared to the stress you could incur driving and parking.

By the way, you may think to yourself that perhaps a trip like this is not for you since you may be in a much younger age bracket than the rest of the group. I look at it in terms of what I can do to reduce the amount of stress in my life. We all know what effect stress can have on your health. Remember the old saying: "Take the bus and leave the driving to us." Day trips, weather they are sponsored by the senior center, AAA, or the local donut shop are a great way to go.

If you are interested in doing some acting yourself, keep your eyes open for local theatre group auditions. In our area, there are several amateur companies that put on productions year round. They are constantly advertising for auditions and for people to work on the sets. Or, better yet, why not start your own theatre group. If there are enough people interested, anything is possible. My wife has forty years of experience in this area. She recommends that a very helpful first step in this process would be to contact the theatre arts teacher at your local high school or someone from the theater department at the local college or university. Perhaps you even can check with the local recreation department of the city or town you reside in.

Concerts

If you live near a University, a variety of concerts await your pleasure. If you are near a concert center, check their schedule. The easiest way to do this is through their website. You may be interested in attending a local symphony concert as well. Check you local newspaper for schedules.

Dance

When my wife and I retired, we decided to get more involved in the art of ballroom dancing. We began taking lessons in the evenings through a local program offered by the town in which we reside (again, part of the adult education course offerings). We've continued taking these lessons and I'm proud to say that our level of proficiency is quite good. I should note that there has been a resurgence in ballroom dancing around the country. A most important consideration here is that you must practice the steps that you learn. A consequence of not doing this is that you will forget those steps. Keep a watchful eye in the local media to keep abreast of ballroom dances that are available to the public. I've found that good sources for these dances are local branches of the Elks Club, K of C, and Veterans Clubs. If you are interested you may also find that there is square dance club in your area. Additionally, you can either burn your own compact disc (if you know how), or buy commercially available dance discs and videotapes (*amazon.com* is a good source) that contain most ballroom dance instruction.

Movies and Movie Clubs

I'm sure that you'll agree that one of the most satisfying things in life is watching a good movie. Unfortunately, it can be difficult to know when a movie is good before you see it. It is sometimes helpful to hear the opinions of others to help you make up your mind. If you want a more critical analysis, you can read the newspaper reviews. Also, you can log on to Roger Ebert's website (*www.rogerebert.com*) or you can purchase his annually updated book of reviews. Rotten Tomatoes (*rottentomatoes.com*) offers a variety of critic and consumer reviews as well as show time links.

If your desirous of learning additional information about a film, by all means check out the Internet Movie Database (*imdb.com*) for facts about cast, crew, directors, producers, release dates and reviews.

The Key Sunday Cinema Club *(keysundaycinemaclub.com)* is a nationally syndicated movie club. The purpose of this club is to preview, discuss, and analyze some of the new movies that are about to debut. This particular club has screening locations around the country. The movie dates are usually on Sundays. I've found this activity to be very stimulating and enriching. Not only do you hear interesting comments by other moviegoers, but also guest speakers are often present. Many of these guest speakers include directors, actors, and writers of the specific movie. In one case, we were very surprised indeed, when the star of one particular movie showed up to make a presentation and receive questions.

Most movie houses offer special package prices for books of tickets. With these tickets you'll be able to go to any show you desire.

Book Clubs

A book club is a simple and great way to share your thoughts with others on a selected book. It's sort of like the Book of the Month Club. It's easy to form and run and can be done at a very reasonable cost.

Gather together a group of friends and present to them what a great idea this would be. You'll want to involve friends who actually are prolific readers. In this way you can be reasonably certain that the selection will be interesting to all participants. Each month (or whatever time frame you prefer), one group member makes the selection and hosts the get together. The host will usually provide some sort of refreshment to accompany the discussion. Sometimes the theme of the refreshments may even relate to the time of year or the discussion at hand. It is also the host's responsibility to research and present some background information on the selection as well as presenting the discussion questions for the group. It is important that the some sort of time frame is established so that people know what to expect before they arrive. It is also important that the group members vary the type of material selected in order to make the club a learning experience. Some people are interested in bestsellers while others may be more interested in the classics.

When you arrange dates for the sessions, leave enough time for everyone to be able to read the selection given the fact that people have busy schedules. This time frame becomes easier for you to set after a period of trial runs. Some research may be necessary in order to come up with the current selection. Consult recommendations from your local bookstore as well as book reviews from the major newspapers.

Creative Writing

I recently read about a retired lawyer who took up creative writing as a hobby. He writes poetic essays and submits them to a local publication for publishing. He finds this to be a very stimulating endeavor along with his other interests, which include painting, and playing a musical instrument.

I really do believe that you can never really know if you are good at something unless you first try it. If you think that you have particular interest in writing, take and adult education course or audit a course at your local university. And, do not forget about the easy accessibility to an online course. After learning the basics, give it a try. You may indeed find that you have a propensity for writing. There are also many wonderful reference books available at your local bookstore to assist you with this.

Museums and Galleries

Most metropolitan areas have art galleries, museums, and historical landmarks for you to visit. In addition, these institutions are always looking for volunteers and part time employees to help out. Check the website for your town, city, and state to find a complete list. Your local newspaper may also list special events taking place at certain times.

I'll never forget in my role as a teacher, how thrilled my students were with the sessions we spent at the Yale Art Gallery (*artgallery.yale.edu/*), in New Haven Connecticut. The guides were simply wonderful in terms of interpreting the art. In particular, the students seemed to have gained a historical perspective of our country, as seen through the eyes of the various artists, that they might have never otherwise experienced. I've found that many people learn better through visual stimulation. If you are one of these people, by all means go to a gallery and be dazzled.

The education department of the Yale Art Gallery offers an ongoing program of art instruction in the schools, in an effort to further increase the students' artistic experiences. They actually will conduct art lessons in classrooms. Further, they offer the use of their volunteers in the schools to assist. I've been told by the administration that many major galleries run similar programs and are in need of art volunteers, just in case you are interested. Remember, you'll be educating yourself as well as helping others.

Transportation Museums

The following museums are examples of Americans love for travel:

- RV Heritage Foundation Hall of Fame, Museum and Library (Elkhart, Indiana) (*www.rv-mh-hall-of-fame.org/museum.html*) - Here you'll get an idea of the technological and chronological advancements in the RV industry with exhibits of the earliest RVs.

- Steamboat Arabia Museum (Kansas City, Miss.) (*1856.com*) - The world's largest collection of steamboat cargo and artifacts are featured.

- Museum of Westward Expansion (St.Louis, Miss) (*nps.gov/jeff/mus-tour.htm*) - This museum opens a window into the nineteenth century the events that are associated with it.

- Wright Brothers National Memorial (Kill Devil Hills, NC)(*nps.gov/wrbr*) - Visitors are treated to an exciting review of the Wright's struggle to achieve what had seemed impossible to accomplish.

- Galveston Island Railroad Museum (Galveston, Texas)(*tamug.edu/rrmuseum*) - This museum depicts the City's rail heritage. It is one of the five largest in the country. Featured are more than 20000 railroad items including a variety of cars.

- National Sprint Car Hall of Fame and Museum (Knoxville, Iowa)(*sprintcarhof.com*) - Sprint car racing is one of the oldest forms of auto racing in the country. This museum tells the story of racing legends with more than twenty-five authentically restored Sprint cars.

CHAPTER 7: TRAVEL - NOW'S THE TIME

How many times have you said to yourself, "I'm definitely going to travel when I retire. "

For whatever reason, travel may not have been a priority in your "previous life." Now that you are in a position to travel, you may be thinking that it will cost a fortune and take too much time to plan. Therefore, maybe you should put it on the backburner.

As I said in the introduction, the emphasis in this book is not on financial issues. However, you may have noticed that many of the suggestions that I make are of a frugal nature. What that means is, I want you to make the best choices with the financial resources that you have available. And, in this age of technology, travel planning becomes less stressful and can potentially save you money.

I'm going to suggest examples of ways that you can travel that are both unique and generally cost effective. (Please understand that I can't help looking at things this
way since one of my college degrees is in accounting.) Once again, you'll need to go online to get the most out of my recommendations. The Internet can provide the best way for

you to find up to date travel prices, as well as quick access to pictures, virtual tours (the next best thing to being there), and movies of where you would like to go.

There are many different opportunities available to you for travel around the country or the world. Depending on where your interests lie, you can go the route of the traditionalist or the explorer. Remember, one of the recommendations I made to you early on was to reinvent yourself. Study the following ideas carefully and analyze which of them sparks your enthusiasm. Then, go for it!

House Swapping

House swapping has been referred to as one of the most pronounced ways of getting a feel for wherever you travel. In essence, one gets the feeling of being at home in a foreign destination.

According to Intervac International (www.intervac.com), a house-swapping agency with listings available in fifty countries (which I will talk more about in the Very Cool Websites chapter), there are several distinct advantages of exchanging homes:

1. Economy - elimination of hotel and possibly even car rental expenses.

2. Education and Culture - improvement of language skills and complete immersion into another culture's lifestyle.

3. Security and Comfort - Live at home while being on holiday.

Most of the agencies that deal with house swapping suggest a vacation of between two and four weeks in duration. Generally, families make an exchange with the understanding that they take care of each other's property, feed each other's pets, and water the plants. Before you actually make the exchange, you will have gotten to know your partners through correspondence and telephone calls. An easy way to examine a house you are interested in is through pictures or movies (both inside and out) sent as e-mail attachments. Many participants actually make an automobile available to each other. A checklist of terms and guidelines is usually mutually agreed to.

AARP has come up with some basic principles to assist you in finding the best swap.

1. Make a wish - Think about what you would like in a home including things like air conditioning, water view, and a garden.

2. Learn the lingo - You may think of the word villa as referring to an estate in the bucolic countryside. Europeans may think of this word as a small house on the edge of town.

3. Check your assumptions - A house that sleeps eight might not mean four bedrooms as much as four beds in one room.

4. Ask some questions - Ask things like what do you see when you look out the windows of your house? Do an exchange of interior and exterior photos.

5. Get references - especially from other families that may have exchanged previously with your perspective swap.

6. Start early - AARP suggests that you begin your search nine to twelve months in advance of your travel. For summer exchanges you'll want to have your home listed by the previous fall.

They also offer some timely advice:

- Set some rules - What about responsibility for cleaning and laundry? What about car swapping? (If you do this, make sure that the registration is available.)
- Cover your bases - A list should be made available regarding quirks of the houses you swap. Also, compile a list of local restaurants and sightseeing opportunities. Ask your swap partner to do the same. Enlist the help of a neighbor to assist your guests with the inevitable questions they may have.
- Keep out - Agree ahead of time about things like contents of the refrigerator, and what is off limits.

In general, house swapping is available in most free countries of the world. Check the Website Directory in this book for a more complete list of agencies. Most of these agencies charge you only a small fee to list your house.

House Renting

Have you ever thought about renting a villa in Spain or Italy? With the click of a mouse you can check out these ideas along with thousands of others, close to home or far away.

Web sites that are devoted to house renting allow you to gather much information. You can download pictures, read previous renter's comments, check dates for availability, and basically do an instant comparison of rentals.

Consumers can search property by regions and include criteria such as the number of bedrooms and distance from the water. The owners or property managers who pay a fee to advertise on the sites usually list properties.

Brian Raub, founder of AlVacations.com (*www.alvacations.com*) says that property rentals can be a very good value for your vacation dollar. "By renting directly from the owner you are typically able to get a property for a price comparable to a resort or a hotel room. But it can accommodate more than two people and it's self-catering. You don't have to go out to dinner each night."

There are a variety of vacation homes available with a variety of amenities. Judging by the number of rental properties listed on the various websites, many people have chosen to rent directly. This may mean more savings to you.

The following are some consumer tips that may prove helpful:

1. Try to book at least six to eight months in advance so that more options are open to you.

2. Expect to make a deposit of about $2000 for a two-week rental.

3. Ask how many people can stay in the property. If a house has a well or septic tank you wouldn't want to overload these systems.

4. Ask about the neighborhood. Ask who commonly rents the property. I'm sure that most families do not want to end up in party areas.

5. Expect to have your references checked, especially if you are renting from a private owner.

7. If you have flexibility in your travel times, find out if the property is available off-season. You may be able to save more on rental rates.

The following websites exemplify a good sampling of companies that specialize in rentals:

*ResortQuest International (*resortquest.com*) is one of a few agencies that actually manages the properties it lists. At this writing there is about 20,000 homes, condominiums, and villas available. The company tries to meet the individual needs of all of its customers. Since they are a management company, they offer twenty-four hour toll-free customer service. Most listing sites make an effort to put customers in touch with each other, and then step back and let the parties work out the details. The problem with that is, if you experience a problem such as dissatisfaction with the environment, there may be little recourse. ResortQuest says that they pride themselves on keeping the customer happy. That may even include relocation. They offer rentals in at least seventeen states, Puerto Rico, Canada, Mexico, and Hawaii.

* First Choice Vacation Rentals (*www.choice1.com*) is considered to be one of the best listing rental sites. They have been in business since 1994. During a recent check, they offered more than 5000 homes for rent. Most of their listings were in Orlando, Lake Tahoe, Hawaii and Mexico. Their site provides an excellent search mechanism, which assists users in making specific, needs based searches. There's also an abundance of photos included.

*The Vacation Rental Managers Association (*vrma.com*) is comprised of a group of property managers in the United States, Canada, and Mexico. Here you'll find comprehensive listings of more than 500 members who represent about 135,000 properties. Their directory is divided by geographic location according to state or province.

*Mountain Home: Montana Vacation Rentals (*www.mountain-home.com*) specializes in home and cabin rentals in the Montana Mountains. If you go to their website you'll be astounded at the beautiful property that is featured.

Don't forget to look at the Website Directory at the end of this book for a list of rental agencies and organizations.

RV (recreational vehicle) Travel

I've owned recreational vehicles for the last thirty-seven years. In fact, I've probably owned about twenty (my wife constantly makes fun of me for this) motorhomes and or travel trailers.

We travel quite a bit and have done so staying in hotels and in the RV. I find traveling in a motorhome to be quite comfortable and indeed, much more cost effective than staying in hotels, especially over the long term. You also experience first hand the physical beauty of our country by camping on its land, especially if you camp in one of our treasured national parks. Further, there is nothing like having your own fully equipped facilities (complete kitchen, clean and private bathroom, and maybe even a state-of-the-art entertainment system) with you when you travel.

For those of you who have not traveled in a recreational vehicle previously, they are basically homes on wheels. There are two main classifications of RVs: towable and motorized. A travel trailer, fifth-wheel, or pop-up, is a camper that you tow behind you, while a motorhome, camping van, or truck camper is a self-driven vehicle. Both can contain all the creature comforts of home including air conditioning, a shower, microwave, a television or two, and maybe even a washer and dryer and a generator. Recreational vehicles can be purchased with simple basics, if that's what you desire. Sizes of RVs range in length from thirteen feet for a small trailer to about forty-five feet for a big bus.

Motorhomes fall into three classifications:

Class A: These are the bus type of vehicles in which living space can be utilized from front to rear.

Class B: This is most readily recognized as a van with a roof that may be raised.

Class C: This motorhome is built upon a van chassis and is most easily recognized by the van front and RV rear.

If you decide to tow a travel trailer, check with a dealer to be certain your vehicle is capable of doing so.

Our experience has shown that the larger RVs are not nearly as maneuverable as the smaller models. On our recent trip around the US we were able to visit even the most remote areas due to the small size of our coach. We were also able to drive into most towns and cities and readily find parking. With this added benefit, it was never regrettable that we did not tow a vehicle behind us. Owners of larger motorhomes are usually left without options if they do not tow a vehicle.

You can learn more about this type of travel from the Recreational Vehicle Industry Association website at *www.rvia.com* or *rvusa.com*. I suggest that you rent an RV if you are interested in trying it. I will discuss RV rentals in the next section. If you are interested in purchasing an RV, read "Get an RV" in Chapter 11 of this book.

The Taylors of Corydon, Indiana are perhaps representative of many RV owners. They are both retired. Recently they purchased a 1984 twenty-seven-foot motorhome with 34,000 miles on the odometer. They used it for a 5000-mile journey to Montana and back. They towed a motorcycle behind the RV for their sightseeing needs.

Despite some problems with mechanical breakdowns, they felt that their first RV experience was a positive one. They were thinking of buying a newer RV that might do better than eight miles per gallon.

Mrs. Taylor indicated that would take such a trip again. "We liked the campgrounds. You get to know people from all over the country. It's a lot different from a motel where you have a room and don't meet anybody."

Many RV owners also belong to clubs. There are RV clubs formed for specific manufacturing models and there are clubs for any RVs. A good source to check is *rv.net*. Here you'll find very informative information on RV news, rallies, driving directions, RV shows, campgrounds, and lots more. You should also check out and join the Good Sam Club (*goodsamclub.com*) (800-234-3450). Membership costs only $19 per year. For that fee you will receive benefits such as free travelers checks, mail forwarding, trip routing, directories, a monthly publication, and an invitation to join a comprehensive road service.

By the way, there are many wonderful publications out there to help you get started with RVing, or further your knowledge, or even educate you about full timing it in an RV.

One excellent example is *Steeles Wheels*. Mark and Donna Steele explain how to pick an RV, what to do with possessions, how to afford the lifestyle, how to get mail, find good campgrounds, and even how to find doctors on the road.

David Humprheys, the president (at the time of this writing) of the Recreation Vehicle Association says that many aging baby boomers are starting to embrace RV's and the RV lifestyle.

One of the reasons for this is the terrorist attack of 9/11/01. "After 9/11, family togetherness, getting away and the importance of being in control became important," Mr. Humphreys said.

"The nation had a crisis and the response was to stay at home, spend money here and visit relatives".

Many industry analysts agree that there has been a change in focus toward doing things in America. American's travel to Europe has been off by as much as thirty percent.

Full-Timing

Here's the ultimate long-term vacation: If you really enjoy this lifestyle, you can do as many Americans do and become a full time RV family. That is, live full time in your vehicle and travel wherever and whenever you like. There are many publications explore this possibility which you can research easily through *amazon.com*. Additionally, there are a large variety of websites to assist you. Just do a simple search entitled "full time rving" on Google and you'll be amazed. People like you, who made the move and are anxious to share their experiences, sponsor many of the sites listed. If you follow the sun to warmer climates during the winter months, you'll henceforth be known as a "snowbird". Snowbirds usually gravitate towards states such as Arizona, Texas, California, and Florida (of course). Most of these people depart colder climate during the months of November or December and either remain in one location or travel to different destinations until April or May.

There are many resort campgrounds that cater to this lifestyle and offer many luxury amenities. For example, Cal Am Properties (*www.cal-am.com*) offers a variety of luxury camps in the Mesa Arizona area that feature as many as 300 different activities and events daily. Or, you can stay in the Quartzsite area of Arizona and camp on a basic level for little cost.

Ron and Barb Hofmeister have been living on the road full time since 1989. Mr. Hofmeister retired then at 58. The family let the lease on their home expire, put their goods in storage, and hit the road. Three years later they sold what they had in storage and have never looked back. Everything they own is on the road with them. They receive all of their mail through a mail forwarding service, and have had no trouble receiving medical care on the road. Mrs. Hofmeister feels a great sense of freedom and adventure. Life has become simpler. The Hofmeisters have written three books about their mobile life including *Living and Traveling Full Time in a Recreational Vehicle*(R&B Publications, $16.95). They also have a website (*www.movinon.net*) that, like the book, offers practical advice.

If you are interested in full timing and would like additional information on working, see Chapter 9 for details.

Join a Caravan

Perhaps you are not quite ready to live in an RV. Another great alternative is to take an extended trip with a caravan. There are a number of companies that specialize in RV caravans. In case you're not familiar with this term, when you travel in a caravan you travel with a group.

Usually, all travel arrangements are made by the sponsoring agency. And that is the main advantage of caravanning:

everything is taken care of for you. You are basically left to concentrate on what you took the trip for in the first place-your own personal pleasure. Usually, one or two "wagonmasters" or agents accompany you. You need not fret over issues like looking for a campsite, making advance reservations, worrying over road conditions ahead and disappointment over substandard accommodations.

Of course there may some disadvantages over this type of travel. If you join a caravan, you're not free to roam around and go where you want. There are also time constraints to consider. Schedules must be adhered to. Additionally, caravans can be a bit pricey.

Two popular agencies that deal in RV caravans both domestic and overseas are Tracks RV Tours (*tracksrvtours.com*)(800-351-6053) and Overseas Motorhome Tours (*omtinc.com*). If you are interested in an overseas caravan, I'll have more to say in the Overseas Motorhome Rental section of this chapter.

If you have the financial capabilities, and enjoy being catered to, then this type of RV travel may be for you.

RV (recreational vehicle) Rentals-Domestic

If you have never traveled in a motorhome and you think you'd like to try it, then by all means rent one. Cruise America (*www.cruiseamerica.com*) is one of the biggest rental agencies. You can also check the yellow pages of your local phone book for RV rentals, or call some local recreational vehicle dealers in your area as many of them do rent motorhomes.

RV rental pickups can be easily arranged at airports through a rental agency. There are several that will even pick you up at the airport in Anchorage, Alaska if you would like to travel in the vicinity.

RV (recreational vehicle) Rentals-Overseas

I recently had a conversation with friends of ours who related some wonderful experiences regarding overseas motorhome caravans. If you have the funds available (it can be costly), and like to have your every need catered to, then this camping experience may be for you.

Once again, one of the most reputable agencies that does this is Tracks to Adventures (*www.tracksrvtours.com*). Our friends have taken a variety of overseas RV tours with them, and have nothing but the highest praise for the class of amenities that the company uses. All the tours are conducted with veteran escorts. They recently attended a tour in Australia and New Zealand and have also been to Scandinavia. This company also features tours to Africa, Alaska, Mexico, and around the US. Depending on where you travel, certain trips include airfare and the recreational vehicle rental. Other trips are priced with the use of your own vehicle. Most trips include some meals. The trips also include an extensive sightseeing itinerary. While many of the trips are overseas and of longer duration, you can partake in a domestic trip of shorter length, such as a Mississippi River Barge cruise for nine days at a cost of about $1000.

The company recently offered a complete package trip (including airfare) for two to New Zealand for around $9800. That particular trip lasted about twenty-seven days in duration. The cost of that trip does become less dramatic when you consider that it is all-inclusive. And, at the same time, you get a chance to explore some of the greatest natural beauty of the world.

If you would rather motorhome on your own in Europe or Australia, and not be a part of a caravan, contact the Overseas Motorhome Rental Company (*omtinc.com*). They offer a choice of either a basic rental or a caravan package. Their website is presented well, clearly illustrating the choices of RVs and the associated costs.

If you have your own RV (either trailer or motorhome), then by all means give this type of travel a try. Or, if you've been thinking about trying the RV lifestyle this is a unique opportunity. Our friends indicated to us that the felt that these travel experiences are a great way to make long term friendships since many of the same people participate these trips.

Elderhostel (again) (*elderhostel.org*)(877-426-8056)

I cannot help but extol the benefits of Elderhostel. What a great idea: learn while you travel.

If you skipped over Chapter 3, or you need to refresh yourself, go back and review the material presented on Elderhostel. By all means go to their website (*www.elderhostel. org*) and read Chapter 14 of this book for a more detailed examination of the site.

You should note that programs in the US and Canada usually last about a week. Overseas programs typically are two or three weeks long. A one-week US program may have prices that begin at $500 and includes food, lodging, and courses.

Transportation costs will not be included and you are expected to make your own arrangements. The cost of an overseas program can be in the range of $3000 due to its duration and transportation costs.

Most accommodations are made through moderately priced motels or college dormitories and charges are usually based on two people to a room.

Please be reminded that these programs are for people age fifty-five and older.

If you log onto the Elderhostel website, you can even go so far as to pinpoint on a map exactly which area of the country or the world you are interested in traveling to. Once you've done that, you are brought to a page that shows the offerings in the area.

Make certain that you register to receive free mailings of the course and program offerings.

ElderTreks *(eldertreks.com)* (800-741-7956)

Experts say that mature travelers (fifty-five years of age and older) are the fastest growing group of consumers in the country. Many tour agencies cater exclusively to older travelers, focusing on stress free traveling. Their attention is geared towards comfortable accommodations, along with health and mobility concerns.

Eldertreks offers land and marine adventures on five continents. A strong emphasis is placed on cultural interaction, and meeting people in off the beaten-path villages. Accommodations tend to emphasize comfortable nights. The company feels that older travelers are less interested in roughing it. For example, a 21-day cultural

trip to West Africa loops through Mali and Burkina Faso with a safari on the Niger River and a trip to Timbuktu. The cost of this tour at the time of this writing was $3995 per person. A quick check of their website indicates pending trips to Thailand and New Zealand.

Bicycle Touring

There are many bike tours available both nationally and internationally. If you're thinking about doing a bike tour, don't be intimidated by your age and physical condition. My wife is in her mid sixties and has realized that bicycling is one her true loves (me being the other). We have done a variety of domestic trips. With some regular conditioning, she has improved her physical condition considerably and has become a very competent stoker (the person riding the rear of the tandem bicycle).

Santana Bicycles (*www.santanainc.com*) (800-334-6136) offers a variety of tandem bike tours meeting the needs of people on all levels of conditioning and abilities. They offer tandem tours that last between four to ten days and feature luxurious resort class lodging and dining, carefully designed routes, cultural interpretation, and exciting off tandem activities. The company even offers to assist you in locating discount airfares. The tours also offer you the choice of shipping your own bike or renting one on location.

A more profound goal that the company has is to "blend the camaraderie of spirited couples with the exploration of an area's landscape, history, cuisine and culture." A recent sampling of the getaway choices includes Tuscany Italy, winter in Palm Springs, California, Pennsylvania Dutch Country, Prince Edward Island, and Santa Fe New Mexico.

The Prince Edward Island Tour, for example, takes place in the fall after the tourists depart in an environment of friendly people, quiet roads, enticing seafood, gently rolling landscapes, quaint villages, along with superb meals, inns and attractions. Now doesn't that sound incredibly enticing?

Senior Cycling (*www.seniorcycling.com*) (540-668-6307) offers two-ten day programs throughout the United States, as well as day trips in the Washington D.C. area. The company caters to the over fifty population. Their tours vary from beginner to advanced levels. The emphasis is not on how far you can go and how fast you can get there. Rather, the goal is enjoyment for all participants. One particular intermediate level trip goes along the Erie Canal from Buffalo to Albany. The duration is one week and the cost is $1260 all-inclusive. This trip averages about fifty-five miles of pedaling each day. Another shorter beginner trip is a two-day tour of the Northern Neck of Virginia and costs about $215.

For your information, there are several companies such as Co-Motion (*www.co-motion.com*) or Bike Friday (*www.bikefriday.com*) that manufacture folding bikes that you can actually take with you on a trip. They pack neatly and easily into one or two cases for transport on an airplane. I might add here that my wife and I recently purchased one of their folding tandems.

If you feel that you are not exactly ready for this type of touring there is another more simple way to go. Mount a bicycle rack on your car and take your bike on easy day trips (of any duration). There are a variety of easy to mount racks available along with lightweight bicycles. If you are new to biking, select a scenic area with easy to navigate roads and you are off. To enhance this delightful endeavor, pack a picnic lunch to take along or stop at a favorite inn. You will feel good about yourself for trying something new and for realizing the benefits of this wonderful form of exercise.

Bike trail maps are generally obtainable from your local tourism department, parks and recreation department, and on the Internet. For instance, if you were going to Virginia Beach, search for "Virginia Beach Bicycle Trails".

Walking Vacations

Given the increasing concerns that we have over our health and our waistline, more of us desire a vacation that includes exercise. A walking vacation becomes an obvious choice with emphasis on the sights, sounds, and smells of the places we visit. You can experience ever-changing colors, sights and sounds of places you visit.

Walking tour companies have seen a surge in growth over recent years given that 18,000 boomers turn fifty every day.

Walking the World (*walkingtheworld.com*) is in its seventeenth season. They feature walking vacations for people over fifty. Trip durations range in length from seven-eighteen days. Levels of difficulty also vary. Most walks may cover a distance of four-seven miles per day on well-defined trails. Trips are planned to such locations as Alaska, Spain, Portugal and Morocco. A trip to Ireland's Clare and Kerry Counties, for example, costs $2195 all-inclusive.

Geographic Expeditions (*geoex.com*) offers upscale walking and hiking trips to such exotic destinations as Patagonia, Mongolia, and Bhutan.

As previously discussed, Eldertreks does offer a variety of walking tours, most of which are overseas and usually culturally oriented.

Finding Travel Deals

Did you acquire that computer yet? Do you otherwise have Internet access available? I hope so! If there is a destination that appeals to you, and if there were a way you'd like to get there, the Internet is your best buddy. Take it from one who knows both professionally and personally. This may be the best way to get the best travel deals. Let me explain why.

The travel industry has suffered some dramatic losses as a result of 9/11 and, more recently, skyrocketing fuel prices. The airlines and cruise ship companies have been offering tremendous discounts on travel services. And, with the continuing threat of terrorism, the number of people traveling is down. Empty cabins, unused airline seats, and vacant hotel rooms are not a good sign to the travel industry. So, discounts continue to abound. Although this trend may reverse itself, you as a consumer need to know how to get the best deals and be able to take advantage of last minute specials. The all-important question is how are you going to become aware of these deals?

Most people think that a travel agency is the foremost source of information. Albeit that an agency can certainly handle all the details, they may not be able to compete with deals offered by online agencies. I recently booked a cruise to the Western Caribbean. The local agency that I contacted candidly admitted that they could not match the price that I obtained from the eBay travel service. I ultimately realized a savings of $1000. Of course it goes without saying that it is important that you deal with reputable online companies that carry major endorsements such as Yahoo, eBay, or Wal-Mart (yes they even have their own travel service now).

Another way of finding deals is to look in the travel section of a newspaper with a large circulation. My experience has shown that advertised specials may be at inconvenient times, sold out, or are simply "bait and switch techniques" in an effort to get you to purchase a more expensive vacation package.

The best source for travel deals is one that is most current. By now, you know that may mean the Internet. With a little simple research you can find the best, most up to date values available. Many of the best buys are offered by the airlines or cruise ship companies and by online travel agencies. As you may know, transactions on the Internet save companies money (less overhead costs) and those savings are ultimately passed along to the consumer.

If you have the capability to take a trip at the last moment, you'll certainly get a great price, especially if you book an entire package. (For great last minute specials check out *site59.com*.)

I suggest that you begin the process by logging onto the airline websites and or cruise ship websites. Or, if you prefer, you can actually phone the company and speak to a live individual. Remember, airline bookings can be held for twenty-fours hours. Then, check out the travel deal sites listed in the "Website Directory" chapter of this book. Make sure that your computer printer is loaded with ink and paper because you'll want to print out similar packages and place them side by side for purposes of comparison. In the chapter on Cool Websites I will examine one of these travel sites.

A Word (or Two) About Airfares

Travel experts advise that things change fast in the industry, as do strategies for finding the best deal on airfares. If you are content with checking prices on the big search engine sites like *orbitz.com* or *expedia.com*, you may be missing out on better deals with discount carriers like JetBlue and Southwest. The big search engines don't necessarily list fares from these companies.

If you are using the Internet you'll find that *travelocity.com* has a great e-mail feature called Farewatcher that lets you know if the fare drops.

Most experts do agree that making plans on a last minute basis can save you lots of money. Log onto *site59.com.*

Here is some additional very useful information. You may have had the unfortunate experience of traveling a long distance on an airplane in a seat that is a bit lacking in knee room. In fact, you may have been able to empathize with your luggage! Well, now you can log onto *seatguru.com* or *seatexpert.com* and identify the roomiest seats with the most pitch. There is a link for each airline and each type of plane in their fleet, accompanied by a description of space.

Finally, these experts recommend that you price flights from the smaller airports as many of the low price carriers fly from these locations.

Traveling With the Grandchildren

If you've done some traveling (in your past life), think of how joyous it would be to share some of those experiences with your grandchildren.

A major benefit of traveling with your grandchildren is the memories that you create for them. Another benefit is the bonding that will take place among all of you.

If your children are busy, this type of travel would be of great assistance to them. Then, of course, when the trip is concluded, the grandchildren return home to their parents and you are free again!

Here are some tips to help make those experiences even more rewarding:

-Money-

Traveling can be expensive. Many retirees have certain limits on the amount of money they spend. Therefore, it becomes important that you don't overextend your budget. When planning a trip, be careful to take into consideration all incidental costs. (toys, books, and snacks)

-Pick your fights carefully-

Kids can usually adapt to new things. Try to encourage the kids to eat new things. But, don't be pushy if they find certain foods to be too distasteful.

-Grandparents are not parents-

When traveling, relax and enjoy the kids rather than attempting to rule them. This doesn't mean that you cannot set limits. Children need to know what is acceptable and what is not regardless of their age.

-Know your companions-

Children change rapidly and so do their likes and dislikes. It may be a good idea to have the grandchildren stay with you a few days before you leave on your trip. In this manner, you all get reacquainted with each other. Children change rapidly and so do their likes and dislikes.

-Keep things simple-

Don't over-schedule the day. Be flexible with your activities. Start early and take a break for lunch, and, maybe even a nap.

Disneyworld

One of the most popular destinations for kids is Disney World (*www.disneyworld.com*). Depending on the age of your grandchildren the problem becomes one of deciding what to see and when to see it. Much depends on the age of the kids.

A six-year-old child may not realize that Disney World is one of four big parks. The child may simply think of the Magic Kingdom as the whole thing. The rest of the package includes Epcot Center, Animal Kingdom and MGM Studios.

*Magic Kingdom - Disney publicist Dave Herbst says "Cinderella's Surprise Celebration is a park favorite with kids. It is a live show presented on the forecourt of The Castle. The amusement rides at Magic kingdom's Adventureland area favor children, with Dumbo the Flying Elephant being eternally popular. Both kids and grownups like the interactive space fantasy in Tommorrowland as they join forces with Buzz Lightyear.

*Animal Kingdom - Kids love this newest theme park because it has the most live animals than any of the other parks. Here they can take an authentic African safari where wild animals roam the savannah.

*Epcot Center - This park is the most adult oriented of all the parks. It features a nightly spectacular, which includes dancing flames and cascading fountains.

*MGM Studios - With movie-themed rides and shows, this park has a lot for kids. The new Playhouse Disney features a live show with character interaction.

Elderhostel

As you've probably surmised, this organization offers something for everyone. As part of their Intergeneration program, a variety of trips and adventures are presented for grandparents and grandchildren. If you go to the Elderhostel website (*elderhostel.org*) you will see how awesome the selection really is. This is another exciting opportunity for you to bond with your grandchildren.

For example, a recent search presented me with a unique winter opportunity to share an experience in Minnesota's North Woods at an ecology program. Or, you could go to Utah to explore underground tunnels. For the more sedate, there are museum programs and trips such as a recent activity based presentation at the Boston Science Museum.

The Grandtravel Program (*www.grandtravel.com*) (1-800-247-7651)

Developed by a team of teachers, psychologists, and leisure counselors, this program is dedicated to helping grandparents create lasting memories through travel. The program advertises itineraries that "stimulate curiosity, encourage exploration and discovery and are fun-filled." The itineraries are supposed to appeal to both generations. They specialize in trips to natural attractions and current interest (museums, cultural attractions, and beaches). A professional tour guide who is familiar with the particular destination accompanies each tour. Accommodations are first class, deluxe, or best available. Another great feature is that they provide counseling for both the grandparent (who'll probably need it the most) and the grandchild.

Rascals in Paradise (*rascalsinparadise.com*) (415-921-7000)

This travel agency specializes in unique and fun trips for families traveling with kids. Their offerings are worldwide including Africa, Alaska, Italy and Fiji. You can even find a kids' divers program that takes place in the Caribbean, Mexico, and the South Pacific. Itineraries are quite detailed on their website.

Hostelling: Travel For the Rest of Us

There are vacations for those of us who are a little disorganized and have limited funds available.

More than one hundred fifteen hostels dot the U.S., according to Hostelling International (*www.hiayh.org).* Prices vary by the season but are generally less than twenty dollars per night for adults and ten dollars for children. While perhaps not luxurious, hostels are not just for backpackers and hikers as the following examples illustrate:

- Lake Itasca, Minn. - Mississippi Headwaters hostel, built entirely of logs, is in Itasca State Park. Private rooms cost about forty dollars per night. There are swimming, canoeing, biking, hiking and nature activities available.

- Crested Butte, Colo. - This is an old Rockies mining town featuring private rooms for rent at sixty-five dollars a night in the summer, seventy-five dollars in winter. A private apartment for six is $180 a night. As well as extreme mountain biking and skiing, there is also hiking, rafting, fishing and horseback riding for your delight.

- Ninilchik, Alaska - The Eagle Watch hostel, open mid-May to September, sits above the Ninilchik River. There are twenty beds with no more than four to a room. Private rooms are thirty-five dollars. This hostel has free gear for fishing and clam digging.

- Montara, Calif. - Point Montara lighthouse and its turn of the century building are located about twenty-five miles from San Francisco. Private rooms cost forty-eight dollars per night. The area is popular with surfers and windsurfers, but there are also bike trails, a whale preserve and whale watching.

Go to Cache Valley, Utah

If you are looking for a nice summer vacation spot, consider the Cache Valley area, about eighty miles north of Salt Lake City. The elevation is about 5000 feet and is surrounded by 7000-8000 foot mountains. The city of Logan is where the State University of Utah is located. Most of the 18,000 students leave Logan and head home for the summer leaving Logan with a big vacancy problem. The University offers a senior Summer Citizen program to help alleviate the vacancy problem and give the economy a boost.

During a recent summer, 800 seniors took advantage of this offer to spend a few months in Logan. Classes geared towards seniors, workshops, and other activities were offered by USU. You do not need to take courses, however, to qualify for the discounts. There are plenty of deals and bus service around the town is free. There are free concerts. Seniors receive reduced rates to attend plays and operas and there is hiking, and picnics and potlucks at the apartment complexes.

If you are interested in this Summer Citizen Program call USU at 800-538-2663.

Tourist Train Travel

When is a train ride not your ordinary train ride? The answer is, when it's a ride on one of the hundred of tourist railways around the nation and the world.

You can see exactly what I mean when you log onto *routesinternational.com / touristtrains.htm.* Here you'll find links to hundreds of tourist trains. There's antique steam trains, cog railways that meander through mountain passes, snow trains, scenic Maine rail rides, farms trains, river trains, and trolley rides, and overnight trips in remote parts of the world that are unforgettable. With this type of travel, you take your time in an effort to appreciate the natural beauty that it affords.

I've listed a variety of additional links in the website directory that relate to all aspects of rail travel.

Vegetarian Vacations

Here's something very unique. Are you a vegetarian? (I am.) Would you be interested in taking a vacation geared towards people like yourself? As an example, there is even a bike touring company in Wales that offers a package. Be sure to check out *www.vegetarian-vacations.com* for further suggestions.

Houseboat Rentals

If you are looking for the ultimate in rest and relaxation, then renting a houseboat may be your best bet. Obvious additional advantages include the enjoyment of water sports, fishing, and the observation of wildlife.

Houseboat rentals are available in a variety of locations around the country and the world. You do not need previous experience navigating one of these boats, as the rental companies will train you. You can count on spending from about $1000 to $3000 a week for a rental.

I suggest you begin your exploration by going to *houseboatrentals.com.* There you'll find answers to most questions you may have as well as referrals to rental companies. There are also clickable links to various rental locations.

You may also want to consider buying a share in a houseboat. This is very similar to buying a timeshare in a piece of real estate. Log onto *windwalkerhb.com* for additional information about purchasing shares of new houseboats on Lake Powell in Arizona.

Windjammer Cruises

You are probably somewhat familiar with the concept of cruising; especially on a luxury cruise ship. The most common destinations are The Caribbean, Bahamas, and Hawaii. If you've been on a cruise, you know the feeling of being catered to. In Chapter 3, I discussed theme cruises: a way to have fun and learn at the same time.

Windjammer cruises are a great way to have fun and be catered to on a smaller scale. You may sail on an historic 150-foot schooner with an average of 125 berths and forty-five crew members. Although the cabins may not be as luxurious as the more commercial ships, the food and the service are customarily spectacular and, the pace of travel may be more relaxed.

One of the most well known associations is the Maine Windjammer Association (*sailmainecoast.com*). They offer four to ten day trips that sail up and down the beautiful Maine coast. There's a six-day music festival cruise, a ten-day whale cruise, as well as a ten-day racing cruise. You'll see lots of lighthouses and whales along the way. Prices are reasonable, most being under one thousand dollars.

Barefoot Cruises (*windjammer.com*) offers you a choice of four, five, or eight-day cruises. The difference here is that these windjammers sail in the Caribbean. Basically, they travel from island to island stopping at locations such as St. John and St. Maarten. Activities include scuba diving, and snorkeling. They offer you easy travel along with good food. The cost of these trips average around $1000 exclusive of airfare.

If you'd prefer to take a windjammer cruise of a shorter duration, especially if you are concerned about your sea legs, there are a variety of companies that offer trips from two hours to one day. For example, Downeast Windjammer Cruises (*downeastwindjammer.com*) offers cruises around the Maine Islands, or, you can go deep sea fishing for fours hours or, you can take the Bar Harbor Ferry from Bar Harbor Maine to Winter Harbor Maine.

By the way, a good site to keep handy is *epinions.com*. You can readily compare prices and reviews of windjammer cruises along with just about anything else.

Finding the Best Beaches

I had difficulty deciding whether finding the best beaches belonged here or in the chapter on hobbies. Since going to particular beaches may, in fact, be a travel destination, this chapter seemed the best choice even though there are lots of people who make a hobby out of exploring beaches.

So, what a difficult choice this is for you to make. If you love to go to the beach, how do you make the right selection?

If you think you'd like to travel long distances, it helps to decide what your interests lay. Are you looking for a family friendly beach, or are you interested in a honeymoon location. How about whale watching or snorkeling? Do you like to collect shells? Or, are you looking for a nude beach?

Log onto the CNN travel site (*cnn.com/travel/*) to check out their recommendations for the best beaches.

Best Beaches (*bestbeaches.org*) lists their choices for the best locations on the southwest coast of Florida.

USA Today (*usatoday.com/travel/vacations*) offers you their beach choices for solitude along with other categories. You'll also find lots of resources such as beach conditions and weather.

Finally, Dr. Stephen Leatherman, Director of the International Hurricane Center at Florida International University, ranks many beaches and offers pictures at his website (*petrix.com/beaches*).

Online Forums: The Way It Really Is

No matter how you like to travel or what type of vacation you're interested in, do you really have a timely feel for what it would be like at your intended destination? Realistically, printed material can be a year or two old. Online forums, however, are full of tidbits from travelers who have had experiences similar to yours. Messages may be posted internationally.

Here are three examples of online forums for travelers.

- *thorntree.lonelyplanet.com* - This site is most comprehensive with thousands of new postings each day. Questions are posed and replies provided for a variety of topics. For example, I found issues discussed about biking in Jamaica, singles traveling to the Dominican Republic, and the most desirable destinations in the Caribbean. There are also a variety of safety issues discussed. Topics for discussion are neatly categorized by country so it's easy to find what you are looking for.

- *groups.google.com* - Here you will find an abundance of Usenet discussion groups where you simply type in the subject of interest. So, if you type in "rec.travel" a large number of newsgroups will appear. Renting a car in Cozumel, snorkeling in Cancun, and travel to Cuba are just a few. These groups are not moderated so just about anything may appear.

- *virtualtourist.com* - This free community site provides a lot of advice. There are quite a few ads but the information that members offer; including must see activities and avoiding tourist traps are well worth the effort.

CHAPTER 8: FIND A NEW PLACE TO LIVE - KEEP ON LEARNING

In the Introduction to this book, I suggested that you think about the possibility of reinventing yourself. Thus far, this premise has been revisited in a variety of ways. That said, here is yet another rather bold proposition on my part.

Are you happy with where you live? Have you ever thought about relocating? Think, for a moment, about your lifestyle and your environment. You may be living in a house that is too big for you. Perhaps your children are grown and gone, and you are living with the "empty nest syndrome". You could be dissatisfied with your current surroundings because of the climate or the lack of recreational and educational opportunities. Perchance boredom has set in. Given the instability of the financial markets, your nest egg may have been mauled. Maybe you're interested in finding a place that is more economical to live and yet offers you some interesting alternatives.

In 2003, *Where to Retire Magazine* engaged in a subscriber survey to ascertain the most important factors in choosing a retirement location. In order of importance, that information is listed below:

1. low crime rate

2. active, clean, safe downtown

3. good hospitals nearby

4. low overall tax rate

5. mild climate

6. friendly, like-minded neighbors

7. scenic beauty nearby

8. low cost of living

9. good recreational facilities

10. low housing cost

11. active social/cultural environment

12. nearby airport

13. major city nearby

14. no state income tax

15. continuing-care retirement communities available

16. friends, relatives in the area

17. full of part time employment opportunities

18. college town with adult education available

I'm going to present you with some material that may encourage you to begin thinking about change. Remember what the old prophet said: "Your best ally is your computer."

Log onto the Money Magazine retirement web site (*www.money.cnn.com/best/bpretire*) to examine their recommendations for the best places to live and retire. These list are updated on a regular basis and reflect choices that comprise both big cites and remote areas. Some of the criteria for selection consist of having a strong sense of community, a low crime rate, nice weather, low taxes, and excellent education. The site also contains some great calculators. You can also search out a city to learn about what it has to offer. At the time of this writing, some of the choices include the following:

- Providence, Rhode Island (*providenceri.com*)- Providence has undergone some remarkable revitalization over the past few years both along the waterfront and within the city. You'll find the fabulous fifteen mile East Bay Bike Path that follows an enchanting route through a variety of coastal areas. Downtown has been redone and it now has a distinctly quaint ambiance about it. Retirees can continue their education through a variety of University programs. Cultural activities abound. Average temperatures range from 28 degrees in January to 73 degrees in July.

- Sarasota, Florida (*sarasotachamber.org*) - Here you'll get the distinctive "fun in the sun" feeling, along with lots of activities. Retirees who settle here say that Sarasota does not feel like your average retirement community in that many young people are intermingled. Money Magazine describes it as Florida retirement without the "old folks" at home feel. Sarasota also spends heavily on education. Its beaches are beautiful. And, you will also find a variety of theatres and museums. Average temperatures range from 72 degrees to 50 degrees in January to about 91 degrees for a high in July.

- Medford, Oregon (*ci.medford.or.us*) - Medford is a delightful western location. The setting is quite picturesque as it is surrounded by the Cascade Mountains and abounds with beautiful rivers and streams for those of you who enjoy fishing and boating. There are also many golf courses nearby. The downtown area was named a National Historic District with many development and preservation projects underway. Average temperatures in January are 38 degrees and July they are 72 degrees.

- San Antonio, Texas (*sanantoniocvb.com*) - There is much more to San Antonio than the Alamo. Colleges, museums, challenging golf courses, Market Square, River Walk, all come with a small town feel. Better yet, there is no state or local income tax and, the average price of a single family home is only $70,000! Average temperatures in January are 50 degrees and in July they are 85 degrees.

- Las Cruces, New Mexico (*lascruces.org*) - An area noted for its beautiful sunsets and great weather, this area has a high representation of Mexican culture in that it is only forty-five miles from the border. There are many Hispanic-themed celebrations. Needless to say, the restaurants are good, the hiking great and the values even better. Your retirement dollar goes a long way in Las Cruces. Temperatures average 55 degrees in January to 90 degrees in July.

- Roanoke, Virginia (*ci.roanoke.va.us*)- It's been said that southern charm proliferates here. You'll be surrounded by the Blue Ridge and Allegheny Mountains, seventeen golf courses, and great hiking. The downtown area houses a concert hall, several museums and the Historic

City Farmer's Market. Real estate values are said to still be reasonable with lots of room to spread out. Temperatures average 35 degrees in January to 75 degrees in July.

- Portsmouth, New Hampshire (*cityofportsmouth.com*) - Albeit this is a very historical area, it is also quite cold and snowy. Retirees will appreciate the highly regarded Portsmouth Regional Hospital and the city's proximity to Boston (fifty miles). There is no income tax or sales tax in New Hampshire and the property tax rate in only 1.9% of the assessed value. You'll also find that federal statistics indicate that New Hampshire is the safest state in the country to reside. The average price of a three-bedroom home is about $300,000. Portsmouth has a repertory theatre and a music hall. And, you can enroll in a wide variety of continuing education classes at nearby University of New Hampshire. Temperatures average about 20 degrees in January to 70 degrees in July.

If you would like to seek out information about retirement communities around the country, then by all means visit Retirement Net (*retirenet.com*). The site maintains a large database of retirement communities. You can search by your desired type of community and the state in which you're interested. Examples of communities include golf, RV, manufactured homes, Alzheimer's, and continuing care.

I also encourage you to log onto findyourspot.com (*www.findyourspot.com*). You will immediately be presented with an online quiz. The results of this quiz should assist you in finding the best place to live or retire.

USA Citylink (*usacitylink.com/*) provides a searchable database of links on travel, tourism, and relocation of cities and states. Many of these links are official city and state websites.

There is a wide selection of books available at both your local library and bookstore to help you find more information.

John Howells has written eleven titles on places to retire both domestically and abroad. *Choose Costa Rica* (Globe Pequot *Press)* provides the reader with descriptions and information about resources there, which make that location an affordable, and safe location for the active retiree. His other successful books include *Where to Retire: America's Most Affordable Places,* and *Choose the Southwest for Retirement: Retirement Discoveries for Every Budget.*

A book that I found to be quite informative is entitled *50 Fabulous Places to Retire in America*. Lee and Saralee Rosenberg have put together a comprehensive guide of the fifty most desirable places to live based on fifteen inclusive criteria. They discuss taxes, services for seniors, crime and safety, transportation, continuing education, real estate prices, medical care, recreation, and more. There are also some terrific tips on making the actual move.

Downsizing With Style

In anticipation of retirement a California couple came up with a plan for "low stress aging" that includes a smaller and more easily maintained home.

Joe and Audrey Vizzard found themselves in a situation that I described at the beginning of this chapter: The kids were gone and their careers as a physician and a psychologist were behind them. They had simply outgrown their 4200 square-foot home. The Vizzards did not feel that they were ready for an apartment or retirement home.

A friend, with similar concerns, suggested an appealing solution: move to a beautifully maintained mobile-home park that was upgrading to manufactured homes. The Vizzards worked out a plan where they ended up with a perfect house for them along with a strong sense of security and community.

With the equity from the sale of their house they had the financial leverage they needed to purchase their retirement home. The Vizzards ultimately bought a lot with an existing mobile home on-site, donated the home to the Homeless Coalition, and received a tax credit. They then ordered a manufactured home (with some custom modifications) to be placed on their lot.

With no monthly mortgage payments, and with a house that basically takes care of itself, the Vizzards relish their peace of mind. Their community is very supportive.

Certainly this idea merits investigation if you are interested. If you find a park that seems to be compatible with your needs check all the details carefully.

There are mobile home guides out there to help you learn more. *Wheelers Campground Guide (wheelersguides.com)* rates and fully describes mobile home parks. If you would like to compare models of mobile homes, *buymobilehome.info/* offers a comparison guide.

The Manufactured Housing Institute (*mfghome.org*) offers information in manufactured housing.

A Financial Tidbit: Reverse Mortgages

I know that I said that financial matters would not be discussed. However, there is one timely bit of acumen that you should know about. This option provides another way for you to enjoy your retirement while you continue to remain in your home.

If you choose to remain in your current home (nearly 15,000 senior homeowners chose to do just that in 2001), or if you relocate and find at some point in time that your funds are too low, there is a home loan process constructed specifically for seniors called reverse mortgages. This program is sponsored by the Federal Housing Administration's Home Equity Conversion reverse mortgage program (HECM).

Basically, you trade some or all of the equity in your home for a monthly payment. The flow of payments is reversed. You would receive a monthly payment that you do not repay until you sell your home and permanently move out. At that time, the funds are repaid along with the accrued interest. The borrower actually retains the title to the home, and there are no new monthly payments to be made to the lender.

Further information is available from the National Reverse Mortgage Lenders Association (NRMLA). Their website address is (*www.reversemortgage.org*) or call 1-866-264-4466 for free booklets.

A Second Domestic Home (An Occasional New Place to Live)

Perhaps you are not ready to relocate on a full time basis. Have you thought about purchasing a second home?

During the 1980's, I owned two vacation homes (successively) in Vermont. I did this for two specific reasons.

First, I wanted a getaway home in the mountains from which I could ski, hike, and in general enjoy a variety of recreation. I did not choose, however, to give up my primary residence because I was still quite happy there.

Second, I had a desire to put some extra cash to work on what I hoped would be a profitable investment.

Many people prefer this idea of traveling between two residences. If you find this idea appealing, and you have the wherewithal, try to find property that you will not have to put a great amount of effort into maintenance.

We have friends that are semi-retired. They own a home in Connecticut and a condominium in Scottsdale, Arizona. Periodically (especially when the weather is colder), they travel to Arizona to warm up. They keep an older car there so there is transportation available, and there are no maintenance worries since the monthly fee covers that.

On the Internet, go the *realtor.com* or any individual realtor website to peruse available properties. In most cases you are provided with the opportunity to take a virtual tour of properties. This may eliminate the necessity of having to do as much shopping around.

A New Retirement Trend: Live Near a College Campus

A fast growing number of retirees are being enticed by a new trend. There are new retirement communities opening on or near college campuses. Many colleges are seeking new sources of revenue and a way to keep ties with their alumni. Retirees are attracted by the college town activities, and the chance to continue learning, and life along side like-minded adults.

There are at least fifty such developments near campuses around the US. Many are located near major Universities like Duke, University of Michigan, and Stanford. There is also a wide variation in the communities. Some are condo complexes, while others are continuing care facilities with assisted living and nursing care components. So, you'd be able to reside in one of these communities from early retirement through your later years. This is a big plus for people who are concerned about burdening their adult children with elder care issues.

Financial arrangements vary with each development. Simply put, the cost is not cheap. For example, condos at the University of Michigan sell for $250,000 to $750,000, and resident must pay a monthly maintenance fee. Regular lectures are held onsite as well as recitals by the music faculty. At Penn State, you can pay $200,000 for the right to live in the development. But you'll also pay a monthly fee of $2600 that includes a nursing and assisted living component.

Retire to a Foreign Country (Expatriation)

If you've done any traveling in a foreign country, think about the number of times you fantasized about grabbing up some great piece of property and beginning life anew. It almost seems that making such a move might keep you young forever.

While I'm not certain of that, more and more boomers may be considering such a move, especially with their lengthened life spans. Many of these people have traveled more consistently, and are more active and adventuresome.

The big question is - where to go? As you probably can imagine, a pleasant climate is an important criteria. The good news is there are a number of countries that offer climactic advantages as well as a low cost of living. The list includes countries such as Belize, Costa Rica, Panama, Nicaragua, and Ecuador. Of course, Mexico is also a location where many Americans relocate.

It appears that many people are attracted to places that they have previously visited. Others have an inner desire to return to the land of their ancestors including countries such as France, Italy, or Greece.

Relocation to a foreign country requires consideration of some important matters.

Experts advise that the first step is to research the idea very carefully. Think about the nature of the people you would like to be around, and your desired weather conditions. You'll also need to determine whether proximity to family doctors is important. To get an idea of what life is really like, read local newspapers.

In many countries it will be necessary for you to obtain a visa. This process should prove to be painless. Also, it is important to understand that you will still have to file and pay taxes to the IRS. Your tax situation, depending upon your income, can become more complicated. It is quite important that you consult with a tax expert who can make you aware of all tax implications. A good tax reference for expatriates is by author Jane Bruno, a tax attorney and is entitled *The Expat's Guide to U.S. Taxes.*

If you have pretty much decided upon one country, it is a good idea to spend several months there to get a legitimate feel for the new environment. A longer period of time will allow you to experience both climactic changes and life around that particular culture. You can obtain some concrete ideas for living possibilities by referring back to Chapter 7 in this book. You'll recall that I discussed "House Swapping" and "House renting" in different countries.

Even when you've reached the stage that you are convinced that a certain location is just your cup of tea, experts suggest that you rent for a while before you buy. It really does pay to be completely secure in your decision before making such a big commitment. Perhaps another area will appeal to you more over the long haul.

Other considerations include how to access your Social Security checks as well as health care.

If all of the preceding seems daunting to you, be confident that those people who have made the move say it's worth the trouble. Think of it as simply another way of revitalizing yourself.

Certainly, the Internet is a key venue to help you in the decision making process as well as the move itself. I've examined and listed some very informative sites in the "Retirement-Expatriation" section of the Website Directory chapter. You'll find comprehensive tidbits to assist you in making important decisions on this matter. Chapter 15 (Very Cool Websites) features a discussion about *escapeartist.com.*

Now, let's take a quick look at some popular expatriation locations.

> * Montisi, Italy - Tuscany: Known for its rolling hills, charming villages and relaxed lifestyle, people often come to Tuscany to cook and study art. It is located just two hours from Rome with more than one hundred vineyards in the area. A visa is relatively easy to obtain. Since this part of Italy has become so popular, real estate can be expensive. However, modest apartment rentals can be found.

* Costa Rica: There are at least 50,000 American retirees who have made this country their home. It is easy to be enveloped by the fabulous landscape (tropical beaches, lush rain forests, mountains and volcanic craters) and the cultured people of this country. Property taxes are low and the average temperature is seventy-two degrees. Costa Rica is known to have one of the best health care systems in Central America probably because their health standards are among the highest in that region. If you would like more information on Costa Rican travel, go to the following website: *www.costarica.com.*

* The Algarve, Portugal: Lagos, in Portugal's western Algarve is a walled coastal town that is surrounded by golf courses, and miles of red-gold beaches. There's cobbled sidewalks, palm trees, a huge fish market and an interesting variety of shops and restaurants. Scattered about are historic sites as well as fishing villages. Recent statistics indicate that Portugal has some of the cheapest cost of living in Europe. Unfortunately, coastal property is rather costly. If you look at property away from the coast, prices drop. At the time of this writing, some

refurbished cottages were available located ten minutes from the beaches priced at 70,000 and 110,000 euro. For additional details about life in Portugal, go to *portuagal.org.*

* The Dominican Republic: This area has been referred to as the best kept secret in the Caribbean particularly if you would like to buy some property. There is a tremendous amount of unspoiled beachfront property on this island. Much of the property is very affordable. Along with that, you'll appreciate the mountains, pleasant year-round climate and the features of a modern cosmopolitan capitol city. Many Americans have discovered its beauty while on vacation and have hence, decided to call it home. During the last ten years changes in government have led to a vital and growing economy.

* Belize: If you are looking for a beautiful coastline cooled by Caribbean breezes, with a location that is only 1350 miles from Brownsville Texas down the east coast of Mexico, then Belize may be for you. The official language is English. You'll be surrounded by Mayan ruins, tropical rain forests, coral reef, and a variety of

tropical birds. Living within Belize are a variety of diverse cultures including a sizeable amount of American expatriots. Those communities exist in Amebergris Caye, Placencia, Cuozol, and the Caya district. It is easy to become a permanent resident, since the new retirement law allows you to remain in Belize indefinitely as a tourist. It is also easy to start a new business there if that is what you desire. Telecommunications are very much up to date. Socialized medicine offers free medical and dental care to all. Belize is said to offer the lowest cost of living in the Caribbean. The lifestyle is very calm. Real estate is definitely cheaper than the US. For example, you can purchase a beachfront lot for as little as $50,000 or a house with 241 feet of beach frontage for $225,000. If are you used to city life with the associated cultural happenings, you may miss the museums, concerts, and theatre. The following website covers just about everything you'll need to know about Belize: *www.belizenet.com*

* Mexico: More and more Americans are retiring south of the border where the cost of living is low and the weather is excellent (although a bit dry in some areas) year-round. Of course, there is the close proximity to the U.S. And, depending on where you chose to live, you may not need to learn Spanish, particularly if you find a community with a high concentration of expatriates. Chapala, which is located an hour's drive from Guadalajara, is a large colony of U.S. retirees. Home prices average about $100,000 in this area. Guadalajara offers a wide variety of amenities and entertainment for retirees and is a little less crowded and safer than Mexico City while offering the charm of a Mexican city. At this writing you could purchase a new two-bedroom condominium in a gated community with a pool for under $100,000. The following websites will provide you with very useful information on Mexican living: *virtualmex.com* is a great site for potential retirees to Mexico with an abundance stuff that you'll need to know. For an online travel guide log onto *go2mexico.com.*

* New Zealand: The environment here is spectacular brimming with beautiful countryside, lush forests, and beautiful vistas. People are open and friendly in the country. English is the official language. New Zealand is located south of Australia (in case you weren't sure) and is comprised of two islands, which are called North Island and South Island. The lifestyle is casual and it is certainly the place to be if you like to sail. A reminder: As New Zealand is located in the Southern Hemisphere the seasons are reversed. December through February is the summer season with temperatures averaging seventy-four degrees in January and forty-six in July. The average price for a home in New Zealand is about $80,000, which by anyone's standards is reasonable.

Feel Confident About Your Move: Tips for Success

Let's be honest about this. If you've lived in the same home for many years, this moving thing can be traumatic and both physically and mentally exhausting. It may mean sifting through years of memories.

Mary Lu Abbott, consulting editor for Where To Retire Magazine (*wheretoretire.com*), has come up with some helpful suggestions to make the move less stressful. She does speak from personal experience having made two long distance moves.

Avoid unexpected moving costs

Make certain that you fully understand the moving agreement. Get bids from three or more movers and do not be afraid to ask questions. If you use a booking agent make sure that he is readily accessible, especially on moving day.

Check your "order for service" to be sure that it contains everything that was in your original estimate. It is also a good idea to purchase additional insurance to cover replacement value of your goods in case of damage. Determine how the mover expects to be paid so everything will be in order when the day arrives.

It is important to have help (friends or family) with you at both ends of the move to check your things as they are loaded and unloaded. You want to be certain that items are inventoried correctly and at the same time, lend an eye toward any damage that may occur by the movers.

Review the inventory and the final contract carefully before signing. If you are concerned that certain items (furniture, mirrors, and pictures) may need special attention to packaging and protection, inquire about it.

There are three major components to consider making that move easier:

1. Make certain that you allow enough time to execute the move. Eight to twelve weeks is advised. Also, create a schedule and modify it if necessary. In terms of packing, if you are doing it yourself, begin the process early because it usually takes longer than anticipated.

2. Since you pay by weight, get rid of as much unnecessary stuff as possible. Donate what you can. I also suggest that you consider having some tag sales.

3. Try to be well organized: Make checklists for everything. Use a record keeping system such as a file box to keep track of all moving related activities.

A very helpful website relating to relocation issues is *monstermoving.com.* There you'll find links to realtors, movers, insurance agents, and even calculators. For further information on long distance moving go to the Mayflower Moving Company website at *mayflower.com.*

Make certain that you also check out *Homefair.com.* They offer tons of useful links to help you find a good mover, compare the cost of living, explore schools in other communities, find a new job, and learn about senior communities. There are also a wide variety of financial calculators available.

CHAPTER 9: WORKING AGAIN

A study sponsored by AARP and published in September 2002, concluded that of the 1500 workers ages forty-five to seventy-four interviewed, sixty-nine percent of these older workers plan to work during their retirement years. More than eight out or ten said that would work even if they were financially set for life. They will work partly because of intangible benefits, such as enjoyment and a sense of purpose. AARP says that some 18 million people fifty-five years of age and older are still in the work force with those numbers continuing to grow.

According to the Herman Group in North Carolina, which tracks work force trends, 309,000 people in the over eighty age group are still working.

It seems that grandfather's image of retirement may have changed dramatically for many people. A great many of us are not quite ready to neither accept nor do we anticipate contently sitting in front of the TV with a beer each day with an occasional trip to the shopping mall. Many new or potential retirees to not envision themselves spending their days at the senior citizen center playing bocce ball, or as Frank from the hit

TV show *Everybody Loves Raymond* did with his time spent at the lodge playing cards and complaining about what ails him.

We hear almost on a daily basis that Americans are living longer, healthier lives. Most retirement studies indicate that baby boomer retirees anticipate being very active and may even return to work doing something radically different from their previous careers.

A survey done by AARP of 1020 pre-retirees who plan to work after retirement indicated by priority, a major factor that influenced their decision:

> need money
>
> need health benefits
>
> stay mentally active
>
> be productive

AARP also surveyed 364 retirees who are working in retirement. Major factors that influenced their decisions are:

> need money
>
> be productive
>
> stay mentally active
>
> stay physically active

For those of you returning to the workforce once again, it would seem that a plan is again a priority. Discussion of three major reasons to do so follows.

I need the money

In consideration of events that have occurred in the financial markets during the last few years, many people are finding that continuing to work is necessary. Nest eggs have dwindled for many people either nearing or already in retirement.

Towards the end of 2004, an AARP study determined that many Americans over the age of fifty have had to change their retirement plans. Aside from downturns in the stock market much of this is due to low interest rates on conservative investment favored by retirees, as well as widespread cutbacks in retiree health benefits.

This study indicates that forty-five percent of people between the ages of fifty and seventy expect to work into their seventies and beyond, with twenty-seven percent expecting to quit sometime before age eighty. Eighteen percent expect to work after that point.

"We've never seen people say they want to work until they're seventy-five years old," says Jeff Love, AARP'S research director. Mr. Love feels that a major reason for this are the losses people have incurred in their 401(k)s.

Since 2000, there has been a drastic reduction in the portfolios of retirees by about $678 billion, according to a study by the Institute for Social Research at the University of Michigan. About 20 million older Americans are relying on their investment income for part of their living expenses, says William Rogers, an economics professor at the College of William and Mary in Williamsburg, Virginia, and a former chief economist for the Labor Department.

In terms of financial needs, Professor Rogers says "It's the higher-income retirees who are seeking out jobs." This is because they have a greater portion of their assets tied up in the stock market

He estimated that retirees that ranked in the top twenty percent in earnings typically had the most assets tied up in the stock market and in pension funds. People who earned in the bottom twenty-percent were less likely to return to work because about eighty-percent of their income comes from Social Security.

An interesting study completed by the Harvard University Consumer Bankruptcy Project found that seniors are the fastest growing group of petitioners filing for bankruptcies.

A separate study by Demos, a New York based think tank, found that seniors over the age of sixty-five were carrying an average of $4000 in credit card debt in 2001, which is double the amount of a decade ago.

Seniors often find that Social Security is reduced when their spouse dies, or, as previously mentioned, that pensions and health care benefits are reduced due to company cutbacks.

For whatever reason boomers return to work, the Bureau of Labor Statistics indicates that the number of people fifty-five and older in the work force has increased by more than seven percent to around 20 million during the twelve month period ending July 2002.

Career experts say many retirees returning to work can expect difficult times ahead. In certain fields retirees may be considered "washed up", particularly in the fields of telecommunications and technology. Here's an example:

Joseph Turner was a senior service account manager at Nortel Networks. At the age of fifty-five, in May 2001, he took an early retirement package. Several months later, after his

401(k) lost about two-thirds of its value, Mr. Turner knew he would have to return to work. After a series of fruitless interviews, he knew he would have to follow another path. He began doing odd jobs and ultimately became a carpenter working about eight to twelve hours a day.

Career experts say that companies may favor hiring younger workers (even though age discrimination is illegal), and they may be wary of investing in workers whose primary reason for returning to work may be financial. Nor do they want to hire somebody who they think is temporary.

The U.S. Equal Opportunity Commission (EEOC) says that the number of bias complaints filed with them jumped forty-one percent in 2002. Sixty-four percent of those complaints were from workers ages forty to fifty-nine years old. It appears that some companies have productivity and cost issues with older workers. Those figures do not reflect the number of older workers that do not bother to file charges.

Of course, this is all compounded by the effects of a sluggish economy whereby higher paid workers may be more likely to be laid off.

For those of you attempting to return to work in a professional position, the following are some professional suggestions:

Dr. Dennis Ahlburg, associate dean of the Carlson School of Management at the U. of Minnesota in Minneapolis says: "Retirees should avoid citing financial troubles as a reason for returning to work. Don't say you're out of money. Say that you were bored in retirement and you want to be an active part of the labor force."

Bill Coleman, senior vice president of *salary.com*, a web site that provides compensation information for job seekers, says, "retirees should accentuate the experience and attributes that they can bring to the workplace. For example, many are willing to work part time and do not need the salaries that younger workers require. Position yourself as a bargain in that you can work on a project basis."

"Focus on experience and level of maturity," he added. "Don't say, 'I'm old, but . . .'." He said. "By doing that you're admitting a defect that's probably not even there.

Andrew Schultz, president of ProUnlimited Boca Raton, Florida, which advises about how to use retirees suggests that technology can be a big hindrance for seniors who are going back to work (particularly if you are a returning pharmacist or in the manufacturing field). He advises retirees to audit a computer course at a local college in an effort to re-gain confidence. (If you recall, I advised you to do the same in a previous chapter). Additionally, this will be of help to you if you decide to obtain a personal organizer to help you cope with any potential memory problems.

Experts (along with yours truly in Chapter 1 of this book) recommend that you establish a regular exercise routine in an effort to combat potential stamina problems. This practice will certainly help you endure the rigors of a full workday.

If you are attempting to re-enter a professional field, another very helpful suggestion is to establish a network of former colleagues and other professionals to call upon for help. Experts say that these people could become valuable resources in terms of specific leads and possible consulting positions.

I'm bored and need to stay active!

If you are simply bored with retirement, the money is not a high priority, and you'll do any kind of work, the choices are simple. Because you've worked so much of your life, work may be an activity you enjoy doing. There's nothing wrong with that!

Many people will tell you that it is difficult to break away from that daily routine. In fact, if you log onto the AARP website, you can chat with others feeling similarly.

In many areas, there are labor shortages. You may be satisfied with spending your work-time as a greeter at Wal-Mart, or a cashier at the McDonald's drive-up.

A neighbor of mine is experiencing just such a feeling. At the moment he is a part-time security guard. Previously, he was a golf course attendant. Before that, he delivered prescriptions for a pharmacy.

All you need to do is read the classified ads from your local newspapers to see all the part-time work available.

I need to reinvent myself!

In your quest to lead a rich and fulfilling life, you could decide that choices include that new career that you've always dreamed about. Perhaps all of that wisdom and experience provide you with great qualifications to transfer to a new endeavor.

A good book for you to read is *Don't Retire, REWIRE*, by Jeri Sedlar and Rick Miners (Alpha Books, 2003). The authors offer their perspective on how to find a work situation that is both rewarding personally and financially. They assist you in finding your "drivers" which are your "personal motivators". Then you are guided into developing an action plan to assist you in fulfilling your passions.

I also recommend that you explore some terrific online resources. I will explore some of these websites in more depth in Chapter 15 (Very Cool Websites).

2youngtoretire (*2youngtoretire.com*) is a great way to begin. The very first thing you are presented with here is their manifesto. Here it is:

Top Ten Ways to Reinvent Retirement:

1. Retire the word retirement.
2. Realize it's a new concept.
3. Restructure your priorities.
4. Renew your zest for education.
5. Revitalize your energy.
6. Rekindle your taste for risk-taking.
7. Respond to new opportunities.
8. Recharge your system.
9. Revisit childhood dreams.

10. Remember, the wisdom to find your true passion is within you.

The site is chock full of useful material and variety of links that will get you going on this challenge of redefining your life. There are a variety of tips on getting started in new careers, starting a new business, and consulting. You'll also be able to read through a database of 70 stories of other people who are redefining their lives.

NotyetRetired (*notyetretired.com*) is a guide to assist you in finding the job you always wanted. Their motto is "retire to something, not from something".

Coolworks (*coolworks.com*) entitles a main link on their page as "Jobs for the Older and Bolder". It lists at least 75,000 great jobs for retirees or potential retirees who are looking for that dream job.

If you go to the Monster.Com website (*www.monster.com/careerchanges*), you'll come upon some wonderful tools for reinventing your career after fifty. There informational links providing useful self-assessment tools and ideas for finding the work you really desire.

Starting a New Business

Perhaps you've thought about opening that new business you've always dreamed about. Your best source for information is the SBA (Small Business Administration). In case you don't know, the SBA is a federal agency that was created to provide free information and guidance to assist small business people. Their website (*sba.gov*) is very comprehensive. You'll receive step-by-step guidance on how to do just about everything. There's links for first steps, a start-up kit, training, counseling, and how to arrange for financing. You can write to the SBA at the following address:

Small Business Administration

1441 L. Street

Washington, DC 20416

For further information in starting up your new business, check out the Website Directory in this book for some very useful sites.

If you are looking to reinvent yourself in terms of a new career, why not put a special emphasis on doing something meaningful for yourself and others, and, maybe even your environment. You may even be able to have some fun while you work.

Many people may look at retirement as a chance to work at something they've always dreamed about. In this sense, money may not be a primary motivator for returning to work.

The first step in the process is to make a list of areas of interests in which you would consider work.

It is important to think about your dream career when doing this. At the same time, it would be very satisfying to have fun while you work.

For whatever reason you've decided to work, here are some additional suggestions that may capture your interest.

Helping to Ease the Teacher Shortage

The National Retired Teachers Association (NRTA), which is affiliated with the AARP, expects that two thirds of the nations K-12 teachers can be expected to leave the classrooms over the next ten years. Therefore, the nations schools are quite eager to tap whatever teaching resources are available. Teachers of math, science and special education will be sorely needed. In an effort to increase the supply of teachers various strategies are in use around the country. Aside from offering incentives to new teachers, an effort is under way to encourage mid-career professionals to make a switch to teaching. Younger retirees with specific backgrounds may also be able to become teachers. Special intensive short-term certification programs are now available around the country.

If you are a retired educator, quality-mentoring programs abound around the country. Veteran teachers are often needed to mentor less experienced teachers. It is also quite likely that you could return to the classroom as a part-time or full-time teacher without jeopardizing your pension provisions. If this interests you, contact the REA (Retired Teachers Association) in your area. To do so, visit the NRTA website at *www.aarp.org/nrta.*

You've heard me espouse the merits of being a teacher. If you're not interested in working full-time, consider working as a substitute teacher. Not only would you be doing some very rewarding work, but also you will be providing a great service for the individual school system. There is a definite shortage of people to substitute. Also, this is a great way of meeting other people. Contact your local school district's personnel office for mentoring and substitute teaching opportunities. Remember, you do not need to be a certified teacher to substitute!

Caretaking Someone Else's Property

Believe it or not, a growing number of retirees are working again taking care of other people's property. Check out the Caretaker's Gazette, the only publication of its kind that readily connects property owners with property caretakers. Seventy-five percent of the subscribers are at least fifty years old.

Many property owners prefer older people because they have a maturity level that equates with common sense and reliability. Typical advertisers in the Gazette include people needing a house sitter while they are on an extended vacation, corporate retreats wanting to have someone on site during vacant months, and national parks requiring groundskeepers during the winter months. Jobs can last from a few weeks to several years.

If caretaking sounds like something you may be interested in, ask yourself these questions:

Are you flexible if circumstances change?

Are you deeply attached to your possessions, in case you have to travel light?

Are you healthy?

What are your special skills?

Working While Full Timing in an RV

If you need to go to work while full timing it in your recreational vehicle, this information should be helpful to you.

There are a variety of reasons why you would desire to return to work while on the road. If you are looking to satisfy a particular monetary need, you'll need to assess what those needs are and how long you intend to remain in a certain geographical location. Perhaps you may consider staying a year, two years, or even longer. Many people stay in an area just long enough to replenish funds for personal needs.

Depending on where you are staying, jobs may be readily available outside of your campground. You don't necessarily have to work in the campground itself. If you do take a job within the camp, find out exactly the nature of your remuneration. Aside from a salary, are you getting a free campsite? And if you are, does it include all utilities? Is a phone hookup and cable part of the package? If you work in a national park *(nps.gov)*, a full hookup site may be provided. Those jobs are seasonal by nature, and often offer the hosts a most rewarding experience. Make certain you find out hours and days of work.

One of the most important assets you may wish to capitalize upon is using any special work skills you have. Among the most popular skills are computer and mechanical. If you are willing to go through some training, tax preparation people are very much in demand. National chains may offer training and refresher courses. And, those jobs can be available year round.

Running a Business From Your RV While Full-Timing

If you are (or were) a professional in the management field, you may be anxious to escape the stress and headaches of management jobs and set out on the road. Running a business from your RV may just be a logical choice for you. Examples of RV operated businesses can include selling merchandise at flea markets, freelance writing, photography, workplace consulting, video production, event production, and even operating an optical shop. Basically, the sky is the limit.

RV entrepreneurs do offer some advice if you think you might be interested in conducting a business:

Make certain that you invest in the proper equipment if you are going to be on the road. This may include a laptop computer with fax and wireless capabilities, a cell phone, a digital camera, and Internet access.

Analyze carefully what you think your needs may be when considering ways to get online. Some people simply hunt for WiFi hot spots while others invest in costly satellite technology that will offer service in remote areas.

If you are going to be purchasing a new RV try to anticipate what your future space requirements may be.

You'll also need to consider things like receiving mail, paying bills and health insurance.

If you'd like more in depth information about working on the road, pick up a copy of *Support Your RV Lifestyle! An Insiders Guide to Working on the Road*, by Jaimie Hall (Pine Country Publishing, $19.95). I'd also recommend *Living Aboard Your RV*, by Janet and Gordon Greene. You can get very useful information on all aspects of full timing from the Family Motor Coach Association (*fmca.com)* as well as the Good Sam Club (*goodsamclub.com*). If you log onto *amazon.com* you'll find an array of books available on full timing and work.

For further information on temp work, please read the following section as it does apply to full-time RVrs.

Temporary Work - a Revitalized Perspective

It uscd to be that when you thought about a temp job, things like dishwashing, typing, or working on a loading dock would come to mind.

Well, with all of the highly specialized skills and the higher levels of education that many of you possess, the nature of temporary work has come a long way.

Nowadays wages for temps may ultimately be higher than you think, especially since employers do not receive medical benefits. There are, however, agencies that offer benefits based on the fact that you work for them a certain number of hours. You'll need to decide whether or not you prefer to remain a free agent. Being a free agent may be particularly appealing to RVrs who move around, or those of you who desire to work on an irregular basis.

If you skilled in specialized areas, it is important to locate the right agency. At the time of this writing there is a need for a variety of professionals (managers, certain engineers and technical people, medical people), and clerical workers.

In an effort to find these agencies start by checking your local yellow pages and newspapers. You can also check websites including *zeal.com, kelleyservices.com, kforce.com, www.manpower.com*, and *www.employment-plus.com* (healthcare). See the Website Directory for a more complete listing.

Relocate to Semi Retire

Here's a unique idea: If you are desirous of continuing to work, and at the same time interested in finding a new place to live, why not find a great place to do both.

Where to Retire Magazine (*wheretoretire.com*) has come up with some suggested locations for you to consider. These areas maintain that their rate of unemployment is below five percent. Therefore, the job market is healthy. At the same time, these environments are quite attractive. Here are some examples:

- Gainesville, Florida (*visitgainesville.net*) - It is interesting to note that 65 percent of this county is forests, lakes, and wetlands. Of course this is especially significant if you are an outdoors type of person who enjoys places that are not crowded. Gainesville is repeatedly vote the most livable city in Florida. There is no state income or inheritance tax. The average cost of a house is $95,000.

- Santa Fe, New Mexico (*santafechamber.com*) - The climate here is hot, sunny, and dry. There is a diverse mix of cultures with a strong sense of community. Also, non-profit organizations are abundant. Santa Fe describes itself as having a fast growing labor force. It is also big on small business. Internet companies are doing quite well. Tourism and government sustain the economy. It is estimated that 10,000 people are indirectly employed in the arts. By the way, New Mexico is known for its low property taxes.

- Tucson, Arizona (*www.futurewest.com*) - Located one hundred miles south of Phoenix, this area is quite scenic. It is surrounded by five mountain ranges. This city is home to the University of Arizona and has its own symphony, opera, and theatre companies. The average home costs only $160,000. Many local workers are in the service industry with science and industry quite popular. These include aerospace, bioindustry, environmental technology, information technology, optics, plastics, and teleservice.

- Corvallis, Oregon (*www.corvallischamber.com*) - This is a college town known for its historic homes, wineries, mild climate, and its arts community. There are more than fifty parks and wildlife preserves. High-tech jobs are very fast growing in the area as well as entrepreneurism. The average cost of a home here is $175,000.

Best Employers For Workers Over Fifty

Annually, AARP comes out with a list of the best employers for workers over fifty. To be among the lucky companies on this select list, certain practices must be evident. These include flexible scheduling, telecommuting, and tuition reimbursement. Many offer more extensive benefits including phased in retirement, skills training, and health and finance workshops.

Clearly, these companies do recognize the valuable skills older workers possess. So, here's their top ten for 2004:

1. Charles Stark Draper Laboratory, Cambridge MA
2. Deere & Company, Moline IL
3. Scripps Health, San Diego, CA
4. Principal Financial Group, Des Moines, IA
5. Pitney Bowes, Inc., Stamford, CT
6. Volkswagen of America, Inc., Auburn Hills, MI

7. SSM Health Care, ST. Louis, MO

8. Scottsdale Healthcare Corp., Scottsdale, AZ

9. Lincoln Financial Group, Philadelphia, PA

10. Beaumont Hospitals, Southfield, MI

Phased Retirement

If you think that you're not quite ready to be fully retired, the process of phased retirement allows the transition to be more gradual rather than abrupt.

Phased retirement allows employees to work reduced hours for a period of time before becoming fully retired. There is variety of reasons for employers and employees to do this.

With shortages of skilled workers employers are prompted to attract and retain valued older workers. These workers (phased retirees) can be used as mentors and trainers of new hires. Additionally, lawmakers favor lengthening people's working years because they will continue to contribute to Social Security.

Employees can now avoid the stressful search for new jobs that allow them to work fewer hours. Ultimately, the transition to full retirement becomes easier.

CHAPTER 10: GET A PET

Do you have a pet? If not, definitely consider getting one. A variety of studies have concluded that pets are good for you. In fact, you'd be amazed how good they actually are.

For example, dog owners go to the doctor less than people who don't own dogs, concluded a study of 1000 elderly Californians. Dog owners had twenty-one percent fewer contacts with physicians than participants who did not own dogs. The researcher, UCLA professor Judith Seigal, surmised that dogs were a stress buffer, which lessened the need of their owners to seek physicians in times of psychological stress. ("Pet Owners Go to the Doctor Less," New York Times, Aug. 2, 1990)

As the owner of two cats, I can, without reservation, state that there is nothing as soothing as the sound of my Persian cat purring as he relaxes on my lap. (I've actually tried to persuade my wife to try this with me but she has thus far refused!) I'd even go so far as to say that I'm close to being in some sort of meditative state.

One of the most amazing books I've read is entitled *The Healing Power of Pets*, by Dr. Marty Becker. He explores in depth how our pets have the ability to keep us healthy and happy in very specific ways. Dr. Becker describes our pets as "vitamins fortifying us against invisible threats". A variety of examples in the book illustrate healing powers in areas like cancer cures, the relief of chronic pain, and alternatives to sedentary lifestyles. His approach is described as one of the most powerful weapons in fighting disease and treating chronic conditions. Many doctors routinely prescribe pets for their patients. Dr. Becker includes a step-by-step guide that teaches pet lovers how to deepen their relationships with their pets for the benefit of everyone. One of the chapters in the book describes how to find the best pet for what ails you.

Another chapter provides a variety of questions for you to consider in determining if you are pet ready. For example, can you afford the cost of pet care, or do you have any allergies that might make owning a pet problematic?

The Sacramento, California chapter of the Society for Prevention of Cruelty to Animals (*www.sspca.org*) maintains a very comprehensive website providing a great deal of information for the perspective pet owner. The following article was prepared by the chapter and should prove quite helpful to you if you are considering getting a pet.

Things to Consider Before Getting A Pet
(Guidelines From the Sacramento, California SPCA, sspca.org)

If you are like most of us falling in love with a pet is easy. Pets give us unconditional love, loyalty, and provide constant companionship. Adopting a pet, however, is a big decision. Dogs and cats are living beings that require lots of time, money and commitment - over 15 years worth in many cases. Pet ownership can be rewarding, but only if you think through your decision before you adopt.

Questions to Ask Yourself:
Why do you want a pet?
Adopting a pet because the kids have been asking for a puppy or a kitten usually ends up being a big mistake. If you have children under six years old, for example, you might consider waiting a few years before you adopt a companion animal. Problem free, responsible pet ownership requires children who

are mature enough to properly handle and help care for your new pet.

Do you have time for a pet?

Dogs, cats and other companion animals cannot be ignored just because you or the children are too tired or too busy. They require food, water, exercise, care and companionship every day of every year. Thousands of animals end up in

Shelters, or are put to death (euthanized) because their owners did not realize how much time it took to properly care for their pet.

Can you afford a pet?

The adoption fee is just the beginning of a lifetime of expenses.

Expenses: (Dog/Cat)

Adoption (at a shelter this includes spay-neuter fee) $80/ $65

Vaccines (2 per year @ 15 each) $450/$450

Heartworm test (1 per year) $25/$30

Heartworm prevention pills (varies depending on size) $900/ $600

Leukemia test N/A /$40

Leukemia prevention shot (1 per year @ $17 each) N/A/$255

Basic health exam (1 per year @ $30 per visit) $450/$450

Microchipping (implanted I.D.) $30/$30

Flea control (varies depending on size) $1,800/$1,440

License ($10 per year if animal is altered) $150/$150

Food (dry) ($182 per year) $2,730/$2,730

Grooming (brushes, combs, shampoo, nail trimmers etc.) $100/$100

Cat Litter ($60 per year) N/A//$900

Litter box and scoop (1 per year @ $10 each) N/A //$150

Collars and leashes $225/$50

TOTALS: dog=$6,940/ cat=$7,440

Please note that this list is based on a 15-year life expectancy and does not include all the expenses you will incur. Don't forget training, illness, toys, treats, bowls, bed, doghouse, carrier, kennel fees, etc. It is estimated that the average cost per year of owning a cat or dog is about $1,000.

Can you have a pet where you currently live and how many times do you think you might move in the next 15 years?

Many rental communities either don't allow pets or have restrictions as to the type of pets they allow. It is not uncommon for landlords to require an additional deposit if you own a pet.

If you might move within the next 15 years, are you willing to move the pet too, and restrict your choice of housing to places where pets are allowed and where they will have the space they require?

Are you prepared to handle accidents in the house, soiled or torn furniture and unexpected medical emergencies?

How will this pet be cared for while you are away on vacation or business?

You will need reliable friends, relatives or money to pay for a boarding kennel or pet sitter.

Is this the right pet for you?

Adopting a large or energetic dog to share your small apartment, for example, is probably not going to be successful.

Some breeds of dogs require a lot of physical and mental exercise, if you are not willing to commit the time and energy required to properly care for these dogs it is likely they will display their frustration with any or all of the following behaviors: barking, digging, chewing or jumping.

Look at your lifestyle and then do some research to determine the pet that will best fit in with you and your family.

Sure, it's a long list of questions and things to consider but a quick stroll through an animal shelter will illustrate why answering these questions before you decide to adopt is so important. Remember, thousands of unwanted animals end up in shelters every year. In Sacramento County alone the average is about 50,000 animals each year. Needless to say, with a number that high the majority of these homeless animals must be euthanized (humanely killed).

Then there is Dr. Rolan Tripp, a veterinary behavior consultant at Colorado State University of Veterinary Medicine. He has developed the "Tripp Tests for Selecting a New Pet". At the end of this chapter I've included Dr.Tripp's test for selecting a new cat. Dr. Becker includes the fifteen vital questions from the Tripp Tests that is a kind of people-pet matchmaking exercise.

By the way, you can tap into Dr. Tripp's website at *www.animalbehavior.net* to obtain more detailed information. A wealth of information is available to you regarding such matters as pet behavior strategies, hints for pet selection, and how to look for the ideal dog. There's also a frequently asked questions link with many useful answers as well as a chat link.

With all of the preceding in mind, you then must decide if having a pet is for you. Are you ready for the commitment and do you have the time? If so, where will you find that perfect pet?

Of course, by now you know that I'm going to recommend that you check some great web sites.

The Cat Fanciers site (*www.fanciers.com*) will educate you on such topics as breed descriptions, cat care, veterinary medicine resources, and cat shows. Make a point to go to some shows to see how your heart reacts to different breeds.

The Dog Owners Guide (*www.canismajor.com/dog*) will describe and recommend breeds based on your needs and lifestyle.

An excellent source for information, especially if you are in the pet contemplation stage is pethelp.net. You can click on training links that are organized by species. The site offers an excellent search mechanism that allows you to pose questions.

The Society For the Prevention of Cruelty to Animals website (*spca.org*) is another great source of useful information with many health related topics.

You can also use the Internet to gain assistance in finding a breeder in your area. Or you can visit a local shelter, if that is what you prefer.

Test For Selecting A New Cat

Rolan Tripp, DVM

Priority   Body Preferences

___ Size: I prefer a cat that is: _ small _medium _large

___ Coat: I prefer a cat with a hair coat that is: _short _medium _long

___ Markings: I prefer a cat that is: _one   solid   color _patterned _tri-colored

___ Grooming: The importance to me of shedding and the "look and feel" of the pet's coat condition. _little _moderate _a lot

___ Age: I prefer a cat that is a: _kitten _adult _senior

___ Gender: I prefer that my cat is: _intact male _neutered male

   female _intact female _spayed

Priority   Mind and Personality Preferences

___ People-Orientation: I prefer a cat that is: _independent _a buddy _lap cat

___ Pet-Orientation: I prefer a cat that will regard other household pets as: _foes _invisible _friends

___ Vocals/Meows: I prefer a cat that meows
and converses with me: _a lot _moderate _very little

___ Vocals/Purrs: I prefer a cat that purrs: _ a lot _moderate
_very little

___ Playfulness: I prefer a cat that
engages in interactive play with me: _a lot _moderate   _very
little

___ Reactivity: I prefer a cat that
reacts to new situations/people by: _disappearing _watching
_joining in

CHAPTER 11: GET A TOY!

I really feel that you're never too old to play with toys! C'mon now, don't you agree? At this point in your life, you deserve to have an adult toy. When you were a carefree child, your parents were probably always telling you to put away your toys. Well folks, now's the time to take them out!

If you have gotten this far along in this book then I figure the level excitement within you has risen and you are probably intrigued that you can actually have some fun in your retirement.

The following suggestions illustrate the kinds of toys that many retirees are interested in. Remember: You should be thinking about living your dreams! You'll notice that I did not include the contents of this chapter in the chapter on hobbies. The truth is, these toys can be rather costly and may not be considered to part of your every day hobbies. You may have the cash readily available to go forward. It is interesting to note, however, that with low percentage financing or even zero percent financing, it may be easier than you think.

Motorcycles

In a recent issue of *Time Magazine* I read an article about baby-boomers attempting to do something youthful and liberating by getting a motorcycle. Apparently it's a phenomenon that's taking hold big-time. A lot you feel that you've done your share of raising the children, paying taxes, and working long and hard. Now, it's time to have some fun and feel young again. A fifty-four year old physician interviewed in the *Time* article indicates that riding makes him feel like he is fifteen again. His senses have been awakened.

I spoke with a gentleman in his fifties who recently ordered a new Harley Davidson motorcycle and actually falls into the above criteria. At time of this writing, the price of the "Road King" bike was $20,000-$25,000. And, this does not include any accessories. I should note, however, that you do not need to spend that much money on a Harley. You can, in fact, purchase a new one in the $6000 price range. Many beginners buy smaller used bikes which can cost as little as $500.

Statistics show that baby boomers are the fastest-growing segment of the motorcycling population. Their numbers have been increasing by 10% per year. Apparently, they have the time, good health, and the financial ability to ride. Increasingly, wives are hopping on back or even buying their own bikes. About one-third of Harley-Davidson owners are now age fifty or older, says Joanne Bischmann, vice president of marketing. Along with this rise in boomer cyclists, manufacturers such as Honda, Yamaha, and Harley are promoting riding clubs.

According to Robert Rasor, president of the American Motorcyclists Association, "more and more boomers are now wanting to try something different in their lives, like motorcycling, realizing they should not put off their dreams until tomorrow". This has been the case even more so since 9/11.

There has also been a substantial increase in the number of people over fifty taking road trips. That figure has increased by about 50%. And, many of these road trips are quite lengthy. Many average as much as 2000 total miles. There are a number of agencies that actually arrange worldwide trips with all trip details included.

If you have never driven a motorcycle, it's a far cry from driving a car. Lessons are important. The Motorcycle Industry Council suggests starting with a two-day course offered by nearly 6000 Motorcycle Safety Foundation certified instructors (*www.msf-usa.org*) (800-446-9227). This qualifies you for a waiver on a motorcycle license test in most states, as well as potential discounted insurance premiums with many insurers. The average cost is $150 per course.

The Motorcycle Safety Foundation offers the following tenets for older riders:

- Because reaction times are slower as you age, keep a greater following distance.
- Pick a route that contains fewer complicated roadways.
- Since eye and muscle movements slow with age, be sure to double-check cross traffic at intersections.
- Make frequent blind-spot checks.
- Use your passenger as an additional set of eyes.
- Choose a machine that has large dials, easy-to-read symbols and illuminated gauges for night driving.
- Wear extra body armor to protect bones in case of a fall.
- Be aware of potential impairment from the effects of medications.
- If older than sixty, have annual check-ups for various eye diseases.

- If you have to stop riding your motorcycle, the Foundation suggests that you console yourself with a sporty convertible.

One of the biggest attractions for the fifty and older biking crowd is the appeal associated with philanthropic biking vacations. The AMA says that there are about 3000 local, regional, and national runs with a charitable component each year. The bikers will usually take donations of money for riding in a parade-like formation. AMA chartered organizations raised nearly six million dollars for charities in 2001.

Here are two additional resources for motorcycling:

* Motorcycle Industry Council (*www.mic.org*) - assistance for beginners

* American Motorcyclist Association (*www.amadirectlink.com*) - provides information on trips and tours, clubs and riding courses.

How About a Classic Car?

Every time I watch an old movie, I yearn to own one of those old cars. How about you? Don't you just wish you were cruising down the road on a warm summer day in your 1955 Nash

Metropolitan Convertible? Or, perhaps you'd enjoy going out to dinner in your 1954 Hudson Hornet Sedan. The reality is that it may not be as difficult as you think to own a classic car.

Just like any other major purchase that you make, it is imperative that you understand the nature of the product. The increased value that is placed upon the vehicle because it is a classic, along with its condition, can substantially inflate the price.

According to the Classic Car Club of America (*classiccarclub.org*), a classic is a "fine" or "distinctive automobile", either American or foreign built, produced between 1925-1948. In their eyes, a classic was high priced when new and was built in limited quantities. Other organizations view classic cars through the 1970's model years.

One of the best places to buy a classic car is Ebay, if you don't mind bidding. *Buyclassiccars.com* and *classiccar.com* are sites where you can also view vehicles for sale. Additionally, there are many classic car newspapers that specialize in private car sales. To obtain the most realistic value of a car that you may have some interest in, go to the NADA website (nadaguides.com) where you'll link up to values of classic cars.

Hemmings Motor News, available in print or online (*hemmings.com*), offers very detailed informational links, as does Yahoo (*dir.yahoo.com/Recreation/Automotive/ Classic_Cars/*). Both of these sites provide great resources to help you educate yourself about these toys.

Other useful resources include *Classic Car Magazine.* All American Classics (*allamericanclassics.com*) is basically a large salvage lot, which boasts three thousand vehicles that are being parted out. You can do business with them online.

Get a Recreational Vehicle (RV)

After all the discussion in Chapter 7 about how exciting the RV lifestyle is, you may have come to the conclusion that you're ready to buy. (Remember, I previously advised you to rent or borrow before you purchase.) In an effort to determine what kind of RV to buy, you'll need to determine the kind of travel you expect to do. Without sounding like I work for the CIA, try to profile your traveling.

Things to consider are length of trips, how often you will travel, and the ages of the travelers. For extended travel or full-time usage, amenities will probably be more important than if you use it sporadically on the weekends. Usually, a reputable dealer can help you with this.

Another very important consideration is your budget. Can you afford to buy what you really want? A question I've always posed to myself is, "Will I get enough use out of the RV to warrant the expense?" Sometimes you can get in on a really good deal when manufacturers offer incentives.

As you probably can surmise, motorized RVs cost more than towables, both in terms of initial cost and possibly insurance. The one caveat here is to be aware of the fact that you need a properly equipped vehicle to tow with. Do not automatically assume that your vehicle is ready to tow. Every manufacturer has it's own towing requirements. And, the process of hitching and unhitching can be rather arduous. I suggest that you observe the process, either by having a dealer demonstrate or by watching someone.

Most experts agree that motorhomes offer a more self-contained experience and offer more of a touring experience since you always have access to the living area. And, if you tow a car behind your motorhome, it's easy to get up and go whenever you want.

The online edition of the RV Buyers Guide (*rvbg.com*) is very useful if you need assistance with the ins and outs of Rving. In addition to complete explanations about the types of RVs, you'll find information on insurance, financing, weights, fuel, and even an RV glossary. Towing guides are available as well as lists of dealerships.

The best time to buy an RV, depending upon which part of the country you reside, is usually from after Labor Day through early winter. This is the time of the year when RV sales are slower.

Obviously, you have two choices: buy used or buy new.

Many great buys can be had if you buy a used RV. Check the listings in your local newspaper classifieds, along with local RV dealer lots. If you purchase from a dealer, you stand a better chance of getting some kind of warranty. Make certain that you do some checking up on the dealer to verify its reputation for service and honesty. Their reputation, especially after the sale, can make or break them. You can do this through discussions with other customers (names which the dealer should readily provide) and the BBB (Better Business Bureau).

Purchasing a used RV (or any other toy in this chapter) from a private seller can have its perils. Certainly the main purpose the seller has is to sell, not service. What that means to you is you'll be buying as-is. And, unless you're careful, that could mean a nasty headache. Therefore, what becomes most important to you is the inspection process. Check any and all service records, and above all, unless you are a handyman bring the vehicle to an RV service center for a checkup. This may be a rather costly endeavor, but it is well worth the expense. It is important to note that appearances can be deceiving.

For a detailed preliminary inspection walkthrough go to *Outdoor Life Magazine (outdoorlife.com)* or RVers Online (*rversonline.org*). These sites offer excellent tips, especially if you are a novice.

You can also choose from a wide variety of vehicles for sale (new and used) when you log onto RV Trader Online (www.rvtraderonline.com) or RV Search (*www.rvsearch.com*). Make certain that before you make that sizeable purchase, you ascertain the value of the subject RV. Again, log onto *nadaguides.com*, or visit your local library and obtain the NADA Guidebook. You can also check out Kelley Blue Book (*kbb.com*) for a second estimate of value.

If you're interested in buying a new RV, by all means attend RV shows to see what is out there. There are great deals to be had at these shows due to manufacturers incentives and dealer discounts. Also, browse dealer showrooms to shop and compare. You can also go to manufacturers websites to view models and request brochures. Go to *rvusa.com/rvmanuf.asp* or *rvzone.com* for links and lists of manufacturers.

Weather you buy new or used there are a few key points to consider:

Be comfortable with things like the floor plan, sleeping arrangements, and storage capacity. It is also important to think about the size of the vehicle and whether you can handle it on the road. Further, the unit will need to have appropriate facilities for the number of people staying in it.

After you've purchased that dream recreational vehicle, you will be free to follow the wind!

Buy a Boat

There are many of us out there that feel right at home on the water. In fact, there are people who actually reside on the water in a houseboat.

If you've ever thought about getting a watercraft, it's important to keep one thought in mind: No matter what your purpose is, there is something for everyone! Whether it's a one-person kayak, or a large yacht, choices abound.

As with any other adult toy we've discussed here, you'll need to consider what your goals are.

Do you expect to take long-term trips, and if so, how comfortable do you need to be? Are you up to the physical demands of maneuvering and maintenance? Do you need to buy a boat that is somewhat portable so that you can take it with you when you travel? How often do you expect to use it? Buying a boat (or an RV) can be a major expenditure. Are you going to use it enough to warrant the purchase price, the cost of maintenance, and any potential storage fees?

As with an RV purchase, the best ways to see what's out there are to attend boat shows in your area and visit dealer showrooms. Again, you will probably find the best prices at a show. If you are new to boating, converse with other people at these shows to gain valuable insight.

There are a variety of useful websites to educate you on boating safety.

The mission of the National Safe Boating Council (*www.safeboatingcouncil.org*) is to reduce accidents on the water and enhance the boating experience.

The US Coast Guard boating site (*uscgboating.org*) offers an abundance of boating safety links along with important reference information regarding boating rules listed by state, navigation rules, federal boating statutes, and boating recalls and safety issues.

NOAA (*noaa.gov*) provides you with marine forecasts.

And, of course, if you are considering buying a used boat, be certain to check the value at *nadaguides.com*.

CHAPTER 12: ELDERCARE ISSUES

Thus far, I've presented you with a variety of suggestions for your retirement that will most certainly enhance your self-esteem, encourage your personal growth, and perhaps even inspire you to have some fun.

I have not, to any great extent, discussed familial responsibilities that you may be faced with. These responsibilities may interrupt your well thought out retirement plan and force you to focus your efforts in a different direction.

Think about your family for a moment. Do you now have the responsibility of caring for someone who is elderly or who has a debilitating illness? Do you think that you may take on this role of guardian or caregiver for a spouse, parent, sibling, relative, or friend in the future? A study published by AARP in November 2002 points out that at least thirty-one percent of the respondents are caring for a parent. Government experts agree that these burdensome responsibilities will increase along with the size of the elderly population. The Department of Health and Human Services indicates that an estimated ninety percent of caregiving takes place at home.

If you are a baby boomer in what is referred to as the "sandwich generation", care giving may even be more difficult for you. On the one hand, perhaps you have older parents that are declining. On the other hand, you may be dealing with you own children and or grandchildren. The result: a very stressful situation is at hand.

In the Preface of this book, I suggested to you how good it made me feel as a public school teacher to affect a positive influence on the lives of others. I also indicated how the Dalai Lama feels that giving to others is a source of happiness. In that sense, having to assume the challenges of elder care may be a good thing for you to do for yourself.

A short time ago, I lost both of my parents within a period of three months. The events that preceded their passing were a most stressful period for me, particularly since I had not yet retired. The responsibilities I had to assume (as an only child) were enormous. I was, however, able to lessen the impact of having to deal with elder care issues with some advanced planning. The following paragraphs will offer some advice based on my years of personal experience.

An important goal that guided my actions through the process was protection of assets. I'm referring to both your assets and the person(s) you will be caring for.

I highly recommend that you consider taking out Long Term Health Care Insurance. The major benefits of this move include the coverage of any long-term major medical care resulting from a catastrophic occurrence or illness. This coverage can apply to nursing home care for a period of time that you pre-arrange as well as in-home services. The Health Insurance Association of America (*www.ahip.org*) offers a free downloadable guide to long-term health care insurance.

When I took out my long-term policy, I did so with a company that was in partnership with the state that I reside in. Therefore, when my term coverage expires, my assets are protected. For example, let's assume that I had a three-year policy and was in a car accident that required long-term care in a nursing home beyond the three-year limit. Upon expiration of the coverage, Medicaid could pick up the cost of my long-term care therefore protecting my assets for my wife or children. Ultimately, you become much less of a financial burden to your family.

I've found some excellent reference websites that will keep you well informed about matters relating to long-term care.

The U.S. Department of Health and Human Services maintains a detailed site containing lots of good articles on long-term care including general guidelines. Many links to associated issues are provided.

The Consumer Law site (*consumerlawpage.com/article/insure.shtml*) presents a broad tutorial with links to discussions on eligibility, contracts, and policies. You'll also find advice on how to avoid fraud.

When you've completed your research on the basics, *Kiplinger's Magazine* (*kiplinger.com*) will help you shop for a company with a variety of comparisons.

When my mother was institutionalized with early stages of Alzheimer's disease, the State wanted my father, who was already living in an assisted living community to pick up the $7000 a month tab. He had limited financial means. If we had done that, he would have had to move to a Medicaid facility and not live the reasonable lifestyle he was living because he could no longer afford the rent.

Through that process, I always felt that he had a right to live the lifestyle he had worked fifty-five years to attain. Apparently, the local Probate court judge agreed. He ruled against the Medicaid claim and allowed my father to live the remaining time he had left in peace.

You may be interested to know that some states now allow family members of Medicaid recipients to receive stipends for taking care of them. In New Mexico, these family members or friends provide basic, non-medical care and receive an hourly rate of nine dollars. Caregivers in this state are required to take twelve hours of training each year including CPR and first aid. The good thing about this approach is that the elder family member is usually quite delighted with this situation because the immediate family member provides the care. Check with the local Medicaid office in your area to see if this opportunity is available.

Taking care of an elderly person requires a large commitment of time on your part. If you share these responsibilities with a sibling, the situation can become even more stressful. One sibling may end up taking charge of things while the others back off altogether. One way to keep the lines of communication open is through e-mail. Reports from doctors or nursing homes can easily be shared as well as personal messaging. This is an especially significant medium when distance or personality conflicts are issues. Hopefully, the team approach will work for siblings caring for an ailing parent. Remember, you can always bring in a professional mediator such as a social worker to help bring things together.

It is important to consider the use of community resources to help lessen your burden.

Errands for a caregiver can be never ending. There's a continual need for trips to the grocery store, the numerous physicians visits, the pharmacy, the Post Office, the laundry, Church or Synagogue, and other odds and ends. If the person is mobile and can travel somewhat independently, there are usually transportation services available from the local senior citizen center.

In many urban areas, the area transit district may be able to provide rides arranged in advance to most destinations for a nominal fee. Taxi service may also be available.

If the person you're caring for has difficulty with mobility, does not drive, and meets certain guidelines, he or she may be eligible for certain community agency services such as Meals on Wheels (*mowaa.org*). (Their website has a searchable database of programs). Home grocery delivery service and laundry pick-up may also be available. If you are greatly concerned about the individual's safety, obtain a personal medical alarm. American Medical Alarms (*americanmedicalalarms.com*) is highly recommended by AARP.

I've previously mentioned that I am the sole caregiver to an uncle of mine who is ninety-seven years of age. As he lives by himself in an apartment, he would be in dire straights were it not for the aforementioned services.

You may find that the community services described in the preceding paragraph are not readily available in your area. Another alternative to explore is that of bringing in a part-time health-aide. I am very beholden to the lovely, caring, and devoted health aide who cared for my parents for two years. The advantages of this service were quite distinct.

Your daily existence as a caregiver becomes much less stressful particularly when you have other responsibilities to juggle. Additionally, you worry much less knowing that the person(s) are eating appropriately, having housework completed, and receiving any required medication. Check your local yellow pages under "heath care" to find listings of home care health aide services.

The most difficult decision I had to make, as a caregiver for my parents, was when the time came to move them out of their house and into facilities. My mother's Alzheimer's was advancing, and my father's physical condition was declining. The health-aide (now living in full time) had advised me that things were getting un-manageable. I came to the realization that there is a point where home care becomes both physically and mentally impossible. An exhaustive toll was being taken on all involved. I remember reading the pertinent advice from physicians who felt that the health of the caregiver and or family members involved might ultimately suffer from the level of stress experienced in these situations. Considering my mother's unpredictable outbursts and uncontrollable behaviors and my father's recurring heart problems I knew what I had to do. I moved my mother into an Alzheimer's care facility and my father into an assisted living community (with a health care component).

Although it may sound like a shameful thing to say, there was much relief for everyone involved once the decision was made.

Long Distance Caregiving

What happens when the person you need to care for lives a long distance away from you, and there are no siblings to share this responsibility with?

According to the National Council on Aging, nearly seven million Americans are responsible for the care of an older relative or friend who lives, on average, three hundred miles away. A major cause for this is demographic trends: many baby boomers relocate away from their hometowns to take jobs, while their retired parents move to warmer climates.

To lessen the impact of distance issues when providing eldercare, a new type of specialist has appeared. Geriatric care managers are trained to address the complex needs of the elderly. They know how to access public and private services and refer families to other professionals. They regularly check on older clients and report back to family members. These services support the older person's ability to continue to live at home. And, if necessary, these caregivers can arrange for institutional care.

It should be noted here that these services could be costly. Hourly rates can range from sixty to one hundred fifty dollars. Of course, the cost is based on the amount of time the caregiver works, which can range from as little as two hours per month to five hours per week. Medicare does not pay for care management although the specific services may be eligible for payment.

If you are interested in obtaining the services of a geriatric case manager, make certain that you do your homework. Research all credentials carefully. Ideally, the manager should be a state licensed social worker, nurse, psychologist, therapist or general care manager. One place to start is the National Association of Professional Geriatric Case Managers (*caremanager.org*). At their web site, you can type in a zip code to assist in locating a manager.

When interviewing a potential case manager inquire about whether the individual has the experience in assessing the emotional, social, physical, and financial status of an older person. The manager needs to be able to keep track of physician appointments, a possible need to hire a health aide and, at the same time, be aware of signs of depression or dementia.

If you think you'll be needing any advice or assistance in these matters, the following websites are very useful:

- *careguide.com* - includes a link for an assessment of elder care issues leading to specific recommendation

- *ec-online.net-* site geared towards care givers with links to Alzheimer's and Dementia information and a residential link and an insurance link
- *www.aplaceformom.com* - provides free assistance with nursing homes and assisted living options in your area
- *www.eldercareservices.com* - a nationwide referral service for elder care living and social services with assisted living and Alzheimer's care
- *eldercare.gov* - (800-677-1116) The National Eldercare Locator assists families that are looking for local resources and answers questions regarding eldercare
- *caregiving.org* - National Alliance for Caregiving offers tips and resources for families
- seniorbridgefamily.com - offers a variety of eldercare resources
- *livhome.com* - a company that provides resources for southern California residents who prefer to keep eldercare services in the home setting

CHAPTER 13: TRY RETIREMENT

Many people have special dreams for their retirement such as touring the country in an RV, moving to the sunny climates of Florida or Arizona, or cruising the oceans.

Yet, some are destined to find that their long anticipated new lifestyles just do not work for them. That recreational vehicle could be too cramped for two. Florida might turn out to be hot and muggy. Exotic cruises may be too expensive and, at times, stomach churning.

Some retirees have found that one way to try to avoid expensive mistakes is to do some trial runs, essentially practice retirements.

Charlie and Lari Johnson quit their jobs in 1994 and spent the next six years cruising the Caribbean in their 53' yacht. Lari, who is 55, feels that a practice retirement is a great idea. "Sometimes people have a whole different perception of what it's like. Take cruising. It's not umbrella drinks on the back deck every night. It's not beautiful sunsets every night."

She said that they met people who spent a lot of money on a boat and, after hitting bad weather or struggling with a mechanical problem for the first time, cruised back into port and put a "for sale" sign on the craft.

You may also apply a similar train of thought to buying an RV. They are, indeed, very costly. It could turn out to be a very confining experience for you and you may feel the driving to be bit stressful. As previously mentioned, it might be more appropriate for you to rent an RV first. Two of the largest rental agencies are Cruise America (*cruiseamerica.com*) and El Monte RV (*elmonte.com*). Try to take an extended trip to see if this lifestyle suits you. If it does, you may want to consider buying a used RV, especially if you are new to RVing. The resale of a used RV is much easier to accept, especially if you have purchased it at a good price.

I suggest that you check the NADA (National Auto Dealers Association) website (*nadaguides.com*) to get the book value of an RV, or boat, or motorcycle, before you buy.

Sherie Corley, who teaches gerontology at Washington State University in Vancouver, says people want to find a place to fit the lifestyle that is compatible with their image of retirement.

"Sometimes they've changed or they're upset with the cost of living where they are, or they want to get away from crime or they're looking for a place that is better fit for their later years," she said. "A lot of them want to be closer to their kids - but not in their laps."

Corley said that one way to try out a new location is to house swap. If you've read Chapter 5 in this book, you'll recall that I've discussed aspects of house swapping and suggested a variety of web sites for you to examine.

"We are in a home exchange crowd," Corley says. "We do it for the travel, but we're finding that some people use it to come to our area, check it out, and see if they want to be in this area permanently.

She says that some retiree relocations turn out to be disasters if they have not thought the move through. "These are people who visit Colorado a couple of times and then build a 5000 square foot house up in the mountains somewhere. Just who is going to visit you in the middle of nowhere? How are you going to get around in winter? What are you going to do when you need medical attention?"

I'd like to add that after our recent lengthy trip around the country, I wondered what one does if one needs a carton of milk?

A reminder: The Internet can supply you with many websites that offer information about a particular location including photos, movies, and virtual tours.

Peter and Evelyn Kearney spent 30 years living in New Jersey before retiring to Florida. After 12 years of enduring near tropical humidity they were ready for a change. And this time they decided to try out their new community before they decided to buy.

Taking advantage of the Del Webb "Vacation Getaway" program, the Kearney's visited the new Sun City Hilton Head site in South Carolina three times before purchasing a home there last year.

"It was so important to us," Evelyn said of her experience "test driving" her future retirement home. " I wasn't sure I would like it. But we came and stayed six days, and it gave us a better feel for the community." She said it was much better than just "coming into a new state with a real estate agent."

At 68 and 72 respectively, Evelyn and Peter are older than many of their Sun City neighbors, but younger than some of them. Asked how they like living in an all-adult community, Evelyn said they love it, particularly since the previous neighborhood in Jupiter, Florida was becoming filled with families with young children.

In Sun City Hilton Head, the Kearneys found their niche. "I'm not much of a joiner, but I like all the things they offer here," Evelyn said, noting her participation in the art club, Bible study group, and her husband's regular appearance on the golf course.

Del Webb, the developer of Sun City and other active adult retirement communities for nearly 40 years, offers prospective home buyers discounted vacation packages, including use of the communities' recreation facilities. Many other retirement communities have adopted similar marketing strategies.

At the Del Webb properties, there's no official sales presentation to sit through. Depending on the location and the season, prices can range from as little as $99 for two nights to about $800 for a week for two people.

The management of this community feels that this package gives potential buyers a chance to mix and mingle with the residents in an effort to find out what it is really like.

Del Webb operates retirement communities for adults fifty-five years of age and older in more than a dozen locations around the country, mainly in the sun belt areas of Arizona,

California, Nevada, Texas, and Florida. Visit the web site at *www.delwebb.com* or call 888-932-2639. For a list of some additional communities that offer trial run packages, see the section in the Website Directory of this book entitled *Retirement Communities* (with trial run packages).

Where to Retire Magazine (*wheretoretire.com*) offers free information on over one hundred retirement communities, many of which offer trial packages. You can order this information directly from the website.

Two other great websites with much information on housing issues are *retirementliving.com* and *www.seniorresource.com.*

If you would like to do a "trial run" on a more simplistic level, here are some suggestions:

Experiment with some of the suggestions I've made in this book:

* Take a course or two in something you've always been interested in. See if the passion still exists. If it does, perhaps a whole new world will open up for you.

* Rent an RV and take an extended trip or two. You may find that this lifestyle is for you and full timing is what you want.

* How about renting a vacation property for a short period of time? Log onto *vacationrentalguides.net* for guidelines and listings.

* Participate in that extended Elderhostel program I informed you about.

Get out and try some of the other activities that I've suggested such as dancing lessons, or kayaking.

After you've done some experimentation, make a practice plan and study it. If you feel that it is jumping out at you and you are excited, then maybe you're ready to go.

CHAPTER 14: TAKING CARE OF MENTAL HEALTH

I've previously indicated to you the astounding number of baby boomers who are beginning to retire. Alas, as these boomers age, along with the millions of veteran retirees, significant personal issues can arise.

AARP reports that over the next twenty-five years as many as fifteen million of us can expect to experience late in life mental or emotional difficulties. That's an incredibly large number.

If you think about it, there are surely a variety of reasons why this might happen. The time may come when one must deal with problems relating to the loss of a family member. Further, the stress of growing older, leading to the inability to continue the same routine may become quite overwhelming. Compounding this may be the incurrence of financial losses (due to the sagging economy or poor retirement investments) that may have severely effected your retirement funding. And, of course, there will be those of you who have lost a job as you near retirement.

Now I'll examine some of the illnesses and disorders that may accompany age advancement, their symptoms, and some commonly recognized treatments.

General Stress

Basically, stress is simply the ways that our body responds to the demands made on it. The effects of stress can include exhaustion and illness (physical or psychological). Since we all get stressed out at times, it is important to understand that certain forms of stress are normal. In fact, some stress can keep you focused and on task.

As for causes of stress in older Americans, most of the common sources are mentioned in paragraph three of the preceding page. Certainly, there are lots of things that can occur on a daily basis that can affect you depending on how sensitive you are. Perhaps you did not receive your newspaper delivery today, or the mail is late, or you're stuck in traffic. Over a long period of time, that stress can disturb your physical, spiritual, or emotional health.

The following are typical symptoms of stress that you may experience:

* Change in sleep patterns

* Loss of appetite

* Elevated blood pressure

* Irritability

* Change in bowel habits

* Headaches

* Back pain

* Feelings of anxiety

* Indigestion

* Elevated heart rate

Too many of these symptoms for too long a time could result in more profound consequences such as heart disease, arthritis, and suicide.

AARP offers a plan for dealing with stress. Their suggestions include:

1. List what you believe causes your stress.

2. How do you think this affects you?

3. Make changes where you can.

4. Do not overload yourself with tasks.

5. Shed the perfection impulse.

6. Set limits for yourself.

Most experts agree on the following strategies to take better care of yourself in terms of stress management.

*Be sure to include, as part of your daily routine, some physical activity each day. You'll recall that in Chapter 2 of this book, I made some specific recommendations. In addition to that, do some housework and yard work (your favorite things).

*Eat well-balanced meals with food that is nutritious. And, take it easy on the caffeine (which can create anxiety).

*Included with that part of maintaining a healthy lifestyle, it is important that you get an adequate amount of sleep each night.

*When you have time, do something you enjoy. Perhaps a new hobby is called for - maybe even something suggested in Chapters 5 or 11.

*Share your feelings with someone you trust, such as a friend, a member of the clergy, or even a mental health professional, if you think it necessary. In conjunction with that, feel free to give someone a hug. Physical contact is considered to be a great way to relieve stress.

*A variety of health experts suggest that you reduce the amount of refined sugars consumed. Excess sugars add stress to the body's physiological functioning because they cause frequent fluctuation in blood glucose levels.

*Finally, try to keep focused on the present. What is done is done! It's very healthful to move on keeping a positive mindset on the present and future.

Depression

At one time or another, we all feel sad or unhappy. That is perfectly normal. However, when those feelings persist over a longer period of time the result may be depression. This is a common illness among older adults. The AAGP (American Association of Geriatric Psychiatry) says that depression can be considered a serious illness and can effect fifteen out of every one hundred adults over the age of sixty-five in the United States. Further, it should not be considered a normal part of growing old. Depression is a treatable illness that affects more than six million people over the age of sixty-five. Many of those affected already have medical illnesses. In fact, depression can exacerbate those medical illnesses according to National Mental Health Organization (*www.nmha.org*). They also say that untreated depression can potentially lead to suicide.

Additionally, serious depression can cause extreme suffering for the individual's family.

When my mother developed Alzheimer's disease, the effect on my father was catastrophic. In his case, the loss of his partner of fifty-seven years led to a dramatic and rapid decline in his physical health. After she was institutionalized, he went into a deep state of depression accompanied by a loss of the will to live. He was waiting for the end to arrive. Unfortunately, medication could not improve his mental health and he died shortly after my mother.

Geriatric specialists generally agree upon the following as possible symptoms:

* Difficulty sleeping
* Lack of energy or fatigue
* Significant weight loss or gain
* Thoughts of suicide or death
* Low self-esteem or feelings of guilt
* Feelings of guilt, hopeless, or worthless
* Persistent sadness lasting two or more weeks
* Withdrawal from regular activities
* Loss of appetite

The National Mental Health Association (*www.nmha.org*) says that sixty-eight percent of Americans over the age of sixty-five know little or almost nothing about depression. And, only forty-two percent would seek help from a professional.

The National Institute of Mental Health (*www.nimh.nih.gov/*) indicates that the lack of action by older people is often based on the feeling that the depression will go away by itself and that seeking help is a sign of weakness. Those views are wrong. Treatment for depression is very successful. More than eighty-percent of persons treated, return to a normal life. Most senior citizens can improve dramatically from treatment. It is imperative that elderly people receive treatment as complications can include substance abuse, medical difficulties and even death.

Most common treatments encompass psychotherapy (commonly referred to as talk therapy). The patient will usually talk to a trained therapist for about twelve to twenty sessions. Discussions are based on specific symptoms. Medication is another approach. Usually this means a prescription for anti-depressants, which can lead to improvement within weeks. In extremely severe cases of depression, electroconvulsive therapy is used. Each of these treatments is based on the level of severity of the depression.

The National Mental Health Association suggests that you first turn to your family physician if you need help. Subsequently, he may refer you to a mental health specialist, which could be a psychiatrist, psychologist, family therapist, social worker, or a mental health counselor.

A group of geriatric specialists, who authored the "Pharmacotherapy of Depressive Disorders" from the Expert Consensus Guideline Series, suggests that there are things that you can do to help yourself recover from depression.

* Try to get out and do things you enjoy.
* Spend time with others.
* Set realistic goals for yourself.
* Progress is gradual
* Avoid making decisions while you are depressed as your judgment may be clouded.
* Things will look better when treatment starts to work.

This same group of doctors recommends ways that family and friends can help: Encourage your loved one to seek out help as soon as possible. And, if treatment is advised, help the individual to stick with the plan. Offer as much as you can in terms of support and affection. Again, try to get the individual out and about doing things he/she enjoys, especially with other people. If the person becomes persistently negative, help him to understand that the depression is causing this.

Refer to the Website Directory in this book for a comprehensive list of helpful websites relating to depression.

Alzheimer's Disease (AD)

The American Association of Geriatric Psychiatry suggests that approximately nineteen million Americans have a family member with Alzheimer's with the addition of 360,000 new cases each year. And, nearly ten percent of all people over the age of sixty-five and up to half of those over eighty-five have AD. Those figures are rather astounding.

The AAGP also says that families tend to care for people with AD until the most advanced stages of the disease have been reached. At some point in time, an AD nursing home becomes the most viable alternative. The cost of that care can range from $40,000 to $70,000 per year. (You'll recall my own personal experiences with my mother in Chapter 12 of this book, and the recommendation that I made that you consider long term health care insurance to help thwart this cost).

Dementia is a medical condition that interrupts the workings of the brain. It is most commonly caused by Alzheimer's disease. What happens is that the part of the brain called the cerebral cortex is affected. This part of the brain controls language and reasoning.

It is important to recognize the signs of AD. The most important indicators are:

1. memory loss
2. language difficulties
3. difficulty in the performance of daily activities (dressing, eating, grooming, using the bathroom)
4. distinct mood changes (agitation, aggression, wandering, combativeness and hallucinations)

Although AD is not curable, treatments are available to control the symptoms and delay the onset of severity. The most common treatments are pharmacological. Ultimately, the treatments may extend the amount of time the individual can remain in the home setting. The AAGP indicates that a person can live an additional eight to twenty-years after the original diagnosis.

I highly recommend that you visit the National Institute on Aging website (*alzheimers.org/pubs/homesafety.htm*) for comprehensive advice regarding home safety for AD patients. There you'll find discussions on weather the individual can still drive as well as weather it's safe to leave him home alone. Home safety tips are offered room-by-room and behavior-by-behavior. Tips for safety outside the home are also suggested.

Geriatric Psychiatrists (something new)

A new kind of psychiatry has recently emerged. Geriatric Psychiatrists specialize in the treatment of mental and emotional problems that effect older people. Unfortunately, because this specialty is so new, there are only about 2600 certified GPs.

In addition to the illnesses described in the previous sections, they also treat substance abuse (including the abuse of alcohol and prescription and over-the-counter drugs) in older Americans. AARP feels that this is an area that is under diagnosed and under treated. Geriatric psychiatrists may often be able to see warning signs that the primary care physician cannot.

They may also be able to detect potential suicide tendencies. Americans sixty-five and older have the highest suicide rate of any age group.

Another key reason why these specialists are so important today includes the management of older people's medicines, particularly when mental disorders come into play. Then, of course, things get even more complicated when physical problems come into play.

Geriatric psychiatrists also specialize in dealing with family members of the patient.

If you think that you may need the services of this type of specialist, refer to the American Association of Geriatric Psychiatry website (*www.aagpgpa.org*). They will provide you with an online referral service, which can be of help in locating a specialist in your geographic area.

A Retiree's Recipe For Happiness

A number of studies completed over the last decade suggest that there may be a way to lessen the impact of some of the issues previously discussed. These studies generally indicate that retirees who enjoy a rich social life with family and friends tend to be healthier. Researchers have found, in study after study, that those people who had more friends were less likely to become disabled and more likely to recover if they did suffer a period of disability. It should be noted that some studies show that people with a broader base of social relationships may experience less heart attacks. In part this may be due to decreased stress. Emotional fulfillment plays a key role in a happy retirement. Gerontologists generally include areas that are critical to this fulfillment: relationships, self-esteem, support groups, life structure and use of time.

Marc Freedman suggests in his book *Prime Time* that retired individuals greatly miss relationships that existed in most work settings. He predicts that more people will look to additional careers to satisfy their social needs.

Many newer retirees want to be with peers who share their values and cultural preferences. They are putting their friends first along with their own emotional needs in an effort to plan for later years.

So, what are their plans? Some older retirees are entering retirement communities with their closest friends. Some groups are capitalizing on the idea of buying land together and building adjacent homes. Still, others who live apart take vacations devoted to the exploration of retirement locations. Some close friends are even checking in to the same assisted living communities when the time comes.

CHAPTER 15: VERY COOL WEBSITES

Assuming you've read the previous chapters in this book, I'll bet that you're on your way to becoming a wizard with your computer. In fact, I'm so confident in your abilities to surf the Internet, you will now be presented with an examination of some amazingly useful web sites. Remember, if you're still a little uneasy about surfing, practice makes perfect. Your computer is your friend and will not express dissatisfaction with your mistakes. The wealth of information available to you out there is readily obtainable with a bit of simple work on your part.

Keep in mind that the most current information about retirement issues is right there at your fingertips. Also, the websites discussed here correspond to most chapters in this book.

AARP (*aarp.org*)

Without a doubt, this is one of the most all-encompassing sites around if you are over fifty-five years of age. The main topical links presented include: Health and Wellness, Learning,

Money and Work, Travel and Leisure, Volunteering and Life Answers.

When one explores the Life Answers link, further choices appear in terms of Care giving, Housing, and Legal Solutions. Current articles features relate to assisted living options, and grand parenting. It is important to note here that AARP is always abreast of current legislation and trends.

I was especially impressed with the Message Boards link. This provides the surfer with the opportunity to discuss, share and learn in their online community.

The travel link offers a variety of travel discounts for the person of leisure, and again, a message board allows you to learn from the experiences of others. Discounts are presented for all modes of travel. For example, at the time of this writing the cost of a cruise to Italy was reduced by $200 to members.

The Money and Work link is very informative. You can read about many issues that effect older workers including features about good companies to work for if you are over fifty.

The search mechanism is very thorough when specific data was typed in.

The cost for joining AARP is very reasonable. At the time of this writing the fee is only $12.50 per year. You must be at least fifty years of age.

AARP Magazine (*www.aarpmagazine.org*)

This site is an offshoot of AARP and is an accompaniment to their monthly printed edition. It is touted as being a "young at heart" site based on the premise that being fifty years old now is not the same as when your parents were fifty.

At the time I examined the site, many of the featured article links involved eldercare. Information was presented on tips for helping your parents as they age. This included important advice on medical care, financial planning, getting through the tough times, and looking after yourself through these stressful times.

There were also links offered on the best companies for workers over fifty, how to re-invent your retirement, maintaining physical health, games, travel, and lifestyles.

The site in is easily navigable with all links well organized. Download times were minimal. Membership in AARP is not required to access the site.

Clearly, this is one of the most useful websites around. The links are very useful in terms of day-to-day life. Material presented covers all aspects of retirement and is geared towards the younger individual.

Elderhostel (*elderhostel.org*)

I've previously described many of the main features of this organization in Chapters 3 and 7. Elderhostel has recently revamped their website. I found it to be more simplified and navigable. Furthermore, if you experience any difficulty with the site, a great online help program assists you on a step-by-step basis.

One of the most outstanding features of this website are it's search tools. When you first load the home page, a world map appears. By clicking on any region you can explore available programs in that country. Or, if you prefer, individual countries are listed alphabetically.

One can also search programs by the type of activity. For example, you can click on canoeing/kayaking, walking, sailing, birding, snorkeling and much more. This feature certainly does offer the potential traveler a chance to have more fun.

If you are at all interested in participation in any of the programs, sign up for the Elderhostel mailings.

I decided to check out two sample trips that were in the listings.

The first traditional trip was to the Pacific Islands (Fiji, Tonga, and Samoa) and was entitled "Tracing the Roots of Polynesia." The duration was twenty-two days and the cost was $5230 per person. The theme was the discovery of the elements of history, culture, and tradition linking these island nations. Participants would explore the arts, natural history, and the economy while interacting with the local Polynesians. Activities scheduled include walking, and optional low-intensity hiking, swimming, and snorkeling. Visitations to museums, settlements, and schools were also schedules.

The second traditional excursion was headed towards Poland, the Czech Republic, and Hungary with the theme being "Central Europe: Past, Present, Future". Part of the exploration was based on a broad-ranging view of these countries in transition. Another trip to Poland was entitled "Teach English in an Emerging Democracy." This type of program was categorized as service seemingly due to the fact that participants would be teaching conversational English to students. It is good to note that no teaching experience was required.

Typical of Elderhostel, many itineraries are not demanding physically and provide excellent educational opportunities for the traveler. Additionally, all travel arrangements are taken care of.

A teaching colleague of mine who had been involved in a number of these programs told me that her experiences had always been very positive and she had always returned enlightened, rejuvenated, and more educated. She truly felt that this type of education was not to be learned from books or college courses. She was afforded a broader perspective on the world and the varying lifestyles of its peoples.

2young2retire (*www.2young2retire.com*)

This has to be one of the most all-inclusive sites that I've seen on reinvention of one's self. In fact, I came across this site after having written much of this book. Much of the information you've gained from this book is quite appropriately complimented in the site. You'll recall that I listed their top ten ways to re-invent retirement in Chapter 9.

The main goal of the site is to describe alternatives for retirement in an effort to encourage you to be as creative as you can. There is a wonderful database of seventy stories of people who are sharing the ways they redefined their lives.

Upon examination of the site, one cannot help but notice how useful the links are.

For example, I clicked on "Getting Started" and was presented with links on launching a business. Contained therein was a list of secondary links and suggested readings that offered the new entrepreneur all kinds of data that would support this endeavor.

A link was also posted relating to going back school. It was there that I discovered that institutions like Harvard are wooing the mature student who seeks a degree in preparation for a different career or to enhance current skill levels. Also, there is much information presented about online course work. A variety of online colleges are featured.

In addition to all of this, links are many links to volunteering resources.

The wonderful thing about this site is that every bit of the information is useful. The links are all active and current, and it is easy to find your way around. It also loads rather quickly which means less time for you to wait.

Most of the data offered from the links is available to you free of charge.

Intervac (*intervac.com*)

This is the site of all sites if you are interested in exchanging homes with another family. The concept of home exchange here involves a vacation exchange for a period of two to four weeks. Since no money changes hands, you're each basically receiving free accommodations. In most cases automobile exchanges are included. The company boasts exchanges and representatives in fifty countries. Many of the member countries have their own web pages, although some are not in English. At the time of this writing they had about 5000 listings.

Intervac provides most of the paperwork for the parties involved to effect the transaction. That would include checklists and agreements. Obviously, a major advantage here is affordability.

You are probably wondering how they make their money. Each Intervac organizer sets a fee for the transaction, which they claim, is less than the cost of a hotel for one night. Fees can range from about sixty-five dollars to one hundred twenty.

The site is quite straightforward with only a minimal amount of downloading time. In many cases you can take a photo or virtual tour of the country and the property. Certainly, this is very helpful in limiting any potential mistakes.

The site incorporates a powerful search mechanism, which allows you search by geography, date preferences, desired time, number of people, and a last minute "hot list." You can also amend your listing, utilize a translation service and pay online.

Intervac offers you two membership options online. Your twelve month membership can be based on the "web only" where you list online and in their book for twelve months. With this option you do not receive a book. The "book and web" option is basically the same thing except that you receive a home exchange book.

A detailed sample listing includes all specifics about the property with some information about the geographic location all accompanied by a photograph. About eighty percent of listings include a photograph because it draws attention to that listing. All photos must be in a JPEG format.

Concerns sometimes arise with members regarding safety issues in terms of leaving one's home to strangers. The company says that since its inception in 1953, adverse reports about this subject have been almost non-existent. A special bond arises between homeowners when you become a guest in each other's home. Constant contact is maintained between families during the preparation process.

WebMD (*webmd.com*)

I think of WebMD as having a doctor by your side offering you medical advice when you need it. Indeed, it is even better than a medical encyclopedia, in that the site is updated very frequently. Therefore, this important information is most current and provides tools to keep you healthy. When I checked out the staff link at WebMD I was impressed by their credentials. They are comprised of a blend of people that specialize in health, journalism, and communications.

Basically they offer you an in-depth presentation of reference health information on a website that is clearly presented. You'll find a variety of links on health updates, and a great symptoms link in which symptoms are organized alphabetically. Of course, their search mechanism is quite comprehensive with information on treatments and medication. The "health and wellness" link brings up material on diet suggestions. Needless to say, it is important that you consult with your own physician before making any radical changes.

Escapeartist (*escapeartist.com*)

If you are contemplating expatriation (retiring to another country) you'll need all the advice you can muster. In addition to the information provided in Chapter 8, I suggest that you log onto escapeartist.com. The links at the site will greatly assist you in decision-making regarding living overseas.

The first thing you should do is to subscribe to their free online e-magazine entitled "Escape From America Magazine." Each issue offers articles written by people who have found their personal paradise. You'll find information about weather, lifestyles, shopping, theatre, entertainment and real estate deals. Contained within a recent issue were best deals on real estate in Costa Rica and Panama, along with info about offshore investing, and opening a bed and breakfast in the Caribbean.

The site offers features on health care, government resources, jobs, commerce, education, travel and banking. All you need to do is click on one of the many countries in the pop-up list and you will be presented with a profile of each country with a discussion on all aspects of living and working there. It is important to note that people like you and I who have actually lived in the particular country have written many of the articles. And, you'll be amazed at the variety of countries that are discussed. The list includes Armenia, Latvia, Croatia, and Moldova.

Refdesk (*refdesk.com*)

This website actually gives new meaning to having "information at your fingertips." The variety of links offered is astounding. Whatever information you require, you will find it here. Refdesk touts itself as being the "single best source for facts on the Internet."

To begin with, most of the online search mechanisms including dictionaries and thesauruses are there. Then there are all of the news and weather sources awaiting your click. You can do a people search, view today's pictures, click on any of the quick find links, check out most major newspapers in the country and examine most major reference tools in the country.

Good Sam Club (*goodsamclub.com*)

The Good Sam Club is a club for RV travelers. At their website the Rv'er will find all the relevant data needed to make the next trip go very smoothly. You'll have to be a member of the club to gain access.

Among the useful information here is a campground reservation system, specific trip planning tools, a bookstore, weather stuff, destinations, events and product testing.

If you are on the road, the site becomes even more useful, particularly if you stay at campgrounds with Internet access. With the addition of their reasonably priced road service component, you may not need your regular auto club road service.

Retired.com (*retired.com*)

This is one of those websites that encompasses just about every aspect of life the retiree would be interested in. On their colorful home page you'll find links to lifestyle stuff, wellness, travel and finance. You can also select from links relating to men, women, seniors, and grandparents. When I checked out the wellness link, I found interesting material on healthy aging.

The men's links presented timely data on sports scores, men's health and clothing styles.

If you are single and interested in dating or meeting new friends, you should click on seniorfriendfinder.com. This is apparently a popular site for people over fifty. Their search mechanism actually allows you to type in specific requirements.

Home and Garden Television (*hgtv.com*)

For those of you unfamiliar with this TV station and its accompanying website, you're missing out on a great amount of information for both the hobbyist and the handyman. And, you'll find that this site compliments Chapter 5 of this book.

One of the links here is the HGTV top ten list. When I explored this list, I came upon some beach craft ideas. One of the things (there were twenty suggestions when last I checked) you can construct out of all those shells that you bring home from the beach is a seashell birdhouse. Step-by-step instructions are provided. There are lots of other craft links including garden ideas and candles. You'll also find tons of decorating and remodeling ideas. Projects are described in detail.

There are a variety of video tours offered at the site. Most of these involve gardening tips.

Gardenguides (*gardenguides.com*)

If you have any interest in gardening, this is a great site to learn from and enhance your skills. Lots of timely advice is offered through the discussion board links. There is a pull down menu listing very complete data on herbs, vegetables, flowers and many other topics. You can also learn when to plant and how to grow better tasting tomatoes. It is also easy to access information on seeds and bulbs. Many illustrations are provided. This is a good site for novice as well as advanced gardeners.

Pethelp (*pethelp.net*)

After reading Chapter 10, you may be considering getting a pet. This site will be of great help to you in how to select that pet. You'll find information on all aspects of selection, care, and maintenance. You can also seek out this information by species. Pethelp offers a search mechanism that allows you to ask a specific question. The results are listed by relevancy to your topic. And, there are discussion forums available to find more personalized answers.

CoolWorks (*coolworks.com*)

As previously indicated, a main link on this site is "jobs for the older and bolder." If you feel that your clear choice is to continue working (either full or part-time), and you are the adventurous type, then this site is certainly for you.

The thousands of jobs listed are updated regularly and are well suited for us retirement age folks. You can readily search out these positions by state and personal interest. Many of the jobs posted are at National Parks during the summer and winter. And, if you have an RV, a campsite may be part of the deal.

A recent check indicated that in Sequoia National Park, a variety of seasonal jobs were available in the following areas: cooks, front desk clerks, auditors, back country camp hosts, retail sales, and maintenance.

How about being a crewmember on a river barge excursion? These are four to ten day trips in which you work a variety of jobs on the barge.

You'll also find jobs at ski resorts, state parks, and a variety of volunteer opportunities.

Monster (*monster.com*)

If you were looking to reinvent yourself professionally, this would be a great site to begin the process. The basic premise here is that you should not have to settle for a job that you really don't want. Although this site is not aimed particularly at the retiree, it does provide you with some excellent tools to enhance your job seeking skills.

A search mechanism allows you to look at over 800,000 jobs by state, listed by category. There's a resume link that offers free advice. You can even pay a Monster expert to write a resume for you.

A link presents tools and tips for interviews, along with suggestions for appropriate dress for the interview. If you need to relocate, you can find movers, rent a truck, and even connect utilities online.

Salaries can be profiled at the site, according to your specialty and the state you select. There's even tips on networking in for your specific area.

Another link offers suggestions on diversity issues and how to deal with them. Monster offers a free newsletter that you can subscribe to.

BIBLIOGRAPHY

Associated Press, "See if Retirement Lifestyle fits."
New Haven Register, 8/28/02

"Baby Boomers Envision Their Retirement: an AARP Segmentation Analysis."
AARP Research, 1999

Becker, Dr. Marty. *The Healing Power of Pets.*
New York: Hyperion Press, 2002

Bronfman, Edgar M. *The Third Act: Re-inventing Yourself After Retirement.*
New York: G.P.Putnam's Sons, 2002

Cantor, Dorothy. *What Do You Want to do When You Grow Up? Starting the Next Chapter of Your Life.*
New York: Little, Brown and Company, 2000

Carter, Jimmy. *The Virtues of Aging.*
New York: Ballantine Publishing, 1998

Cohen, Gene. *Awakening Human Potential in the Second Half of Life.*
New York: HarperCollins, 2004

Cullinane, Jan and Fitzgerald Cathy. *The New Retirement.*
New York: Rodale Press, 2004

Knorr, Rosanne. *The Grown-Up's Guide to Retiring Abroad.*
California: Ten Speed Press, 2001

Laura Koss-Feder. "Saddling Up."
Time Magazine,October, 2002

McCants and Robert. *Retire to Fun and Freedom.*
New York: Warner Books, 1990

Newman, Betsy Kyte. *Retiring as a Career, Making the Most of Your Retirement.*
Connecticut: Praeger Publishers, 2003

Nolan, William. "Downsized With Style."
Better Homes and Gardens, October, 2002

"Pet Owners Go to the Doctor Less."
New York Times, Aug. 2, 1990

Philadelphia, Desa. " Roughing it Gently"
Time Magazine, 8/26/02

Rosenberg, Lee and Sarilee. *50 Fabulous Place to Retire in America.*
New Jersey: Career Press, 1996

Sher, Barbara. *It's Only Too Late If You Don't Start Now.*
New York: Delacorte Press, 1998

Silver, Don. *65 Ways to protect your future, Baby Boomer Retirement.*
New York: Adams Hall Publishing, 1998

Steele, Mark and Donna. *Steeles on Wheels.*
Virginia: Capitol Books, 2002

Wagner, Tricia and Day, Barbara. *How to Enjoy Your Retirement, Activities From A-Z.*
Massachusetts: Vanderwyk and Burnham, 1998

Waldmen, Adele. "Virtual Summer Vacation."
New Haven Register, 5/13/02

Warner, Ralph. *Get a Life.*
California: Nolo Press, 1997

Wasik, John F. *10 Step Plan for Reinventing Your Retirement, Retire Early, and Live the Life You Want Now.*
New York: Henry Holt and Company, 1999

Williams, Wendy. *Best Bike Paths of New England.*
New York: Simon and Schuster, 1996

Zelinski, Ernie. *The Joy of Not Working.*
California: Ten Speed Press, 1997

WEB SITE DIRECTORY

RESOURCES:

General

elderhostel.org - wonderful educational, travel, and social opportunities.

www.archive.org - an archive of over 10 billion web pages (internet archive)

www.delphion.com - a resource for patents pending

citysearch.com - comprehensive search mechanism relating to tourist information for most cities

britannica.com - Britannica encyclopedia online

reversemortgage.org - National Reverse Mortgage Lenders Association

Retired Professionals

cll.emory.edu - Emory University Center for Lifelong Learning

nsu.newschool.edu/irp/ - Institute for Retired Professionals

score.org - professional volunteers counsel small businesses

aarp.org/nrta - National Retired Teachers Association

aarp.org/forprofessionals/ - AARP retired professionals web page

Working After Fifty:

notyetretired.com - information regarding retiring to some new endeavors

www.2young2retire.com - offers a variety of links to encourage you try a new vocation

coolworks.com - a listing of at least 75,000 cool jobs for "older and bolder" folks.

aarp.org/careers - very useful links for retirees wishing to continue to work

monster.com/ - great tools including self-assessment, career changes, and relocation for workers over 50

maturityworks.org - national program that matches mature workers with jobs

www.kelleyservices.com

manpower.com

employment-plus.com - health care industry work

www.kforce.com

zeal.com - offers a list of temp agencies

www.crosscountrytravcorps.com

www.airetel.com - technical and engineering jobs

laborworksusa.com - industrial jobs

www.accountemps.com - jobs in accounting and finance

Starting a Small Business

www.sba.gov - (Small Business Administration) free information and provided by the federal government

www.business.gov - a reference site run by the SBA on laws, regulations, and loan programs

www.bcentral.com - Microsoft's site on tools for small businesses

www.entreworld.org - search engine for topics on start-up

www.startupjournal.com - articles from the Wall Street Journal

Retirement

www.retired.com - great links for shopping, books, travel, chat, and lifestyles)

seniorresource.com - housing options, retirement information

aarp.org - AARP - wonderful site with information on every aspect of retirement including a variety of advice from various professionals.

www.retireearlyhomepage.com - great resource for early retirees

www.backrest.com - retirement book reviews available here

www.seniornet.org - one of most comprehensive retirement sites I've seen, includes such links as book clubs, computer instruction, and investing advice.

www.aarp.org/nrta- National Retired Teachers Association, offering great retirement tools

retirementwithapurpose.com - offers a large amount of helpful retirement links including a wide hobby selection

Retirement Locations (mainly domestic)

www.money.cnn.com/best/bpretire - Money Magazine's best places to retire.

www.findyourspot.com - a quiz to assist you in your search for the best place to retire

retirementliving.com - retirement communities, taxes by state, more

retirenet.com - descriptions of retirement communities around the country

monstermoving.com - a site full of helpful links relating to moving

wheretoretire.com - Where to Retire Magazine

seniorresource.com - a variety of senior resources

Retirement Communities (with trial run packages)

www.delwebb.com - nationwide retirement communities w/trial run packages

thelandings.com - Skidway Island near Savannah, Georgia

laspalmasgrand.com - adult community in Arizona

www.rainbowsprings.cc - custom homes in Dunnellon, Florida

www.chamber.caverns.com - affordable retirement in Carlsbad, NM

jensencommunities.com - twenty-seven communities for adults over the age of fifty=five

www.solivita.com - Orlando, Florida

Expatriation

aaro-intl.org - much information for U.S. citizens living abroad

liveabroad.com - a major help for expatriates including listing for jobs and real estate

www.internationalliving.com - offers great deals in other countries

expatexchange.com- all matters relating to expatriation

escapeartist.com - guiding premise here is live where you want how you want *embassyworld.com* - complete listing of embassies around the world

expatforum.com - a chat room for expats with participation from twenty-four countries

virtualmex.com - a great site for the potential Mexican retiree

go2mexico.com - an online Mexican travel guide.

bestplaces.net - Sterling's guide for best places to live and work

bestretirementspots.com - useful guide to finding the best retirement location

Relocation Sites

monstermoving.monster.com - lots of helpful links if you are considering relocation

homefair.com - a variety of calculators are presented to assist you in costs of moving

mayflower.com - the moving company site that helps you to determine associated costs

Pets

www.animalbehavior.net - Dr. Rolan Tripp's site exploring animal behaviors and their effects upon us

www.fanciers.com - Cat fanciers site

www.canismajor.com - Dog Owners Guide

pethelp.net - excellent source for training and posing questions

spca.org - Society For the Prevention of Cruelty to Animals

Medical

www.webmd.com - clinical trial listings and self-care guides

www.mdadvice.com - medical information database

tmvc.com.au/ - medical advice for overseas travel

medlineplus.gov - contains a wealth of information from the National Library of Medicine

mayoclinic.com - searchable database of information

Mental Health

aagpgpa.org - American Association of Geriatric Psychiatrists

nmha.org - National Mental Health Association

nimh.nih.gov - National Institute for Mental Health

alzheimers.org - National Institute on Aging

www.nami.org - National Alliance for the Mentally Ill

www.DBSAlliance.org - Depression and Bipolar Alliance

depression.org - National Foundation for Depressive Illness

Eldercare

www.ec-online.net - caregivers site relating to Alzheimer's and dementia

www.aplaceformom.com - free assistance with nursing home and assisted living options

eldercareservices.com - nationwide referral service

eldercare.gov - National Eldercare Locator for resources

caregiving.org - National Alliance for Caregiving

seniorbridgefamily.com - a variety of eldercare resources

livhome.com - information for Southern California residents who prefer to keep eldercare services at home

careguide.com - links for eldercare issues

moaa.org - Meals on Wheels

ahip.org - long-term health care guide

americanmedicalalarms.com - personal alarm service recommended by AARP

familycareamerica.com - a wealth of links for family caregivers

nahc.org - information on home care agencies

agingnets.com - geriatric social workers who serve as care managers for aging parents

caps4caregivers.org - resources for caregivers

www.caregiver.org - Family Caregiver Alliance

seniorworld.com/health/health_caregiving - resources for senior caregiving

Older Driver Education and Safety

aarp.org/life/drive - help in locating AARP driver refresher courses near you

aaa.com - American Automobile Association driver safety advice

nhtsa.dot.gov/people/injury/olddrive - National Highway Safety Transportation Administration's advice to older drivers

seniordrivers.org - privately run offering safety tips to senior drivers

*thehartford.com/*talk with older drivers - strategies for getting at risk drivers off the road

granddriver.info - alternative transportation options

Bereavement Links

griefnet.org - online support for people dealing with grief and loss

growthhouse.org - information on end-of-life care

death-dying.com - online grief support by volunteers

aarp.org/griefandloss/home - very informative AARP site

nhpco.org - A Hospice sponsored site

dyingwell.org - resources from a pallative care phyisician and author

SEARCH ENGINES

General:

about.com

altavista.com

aol.com

www.ask.com - Ask Jeeves

www.dogpile.com

google.com (PC World Magazine rates this engine the best)

www.lycos.com

www.metacrawler.com

www.msn.com - (Microsoft - in case you didn't know)

www.yahoo.com (also rated very highly by PC World Magazine)

go.com - all-inclusive search engine sponsored by Disney

Special Search Engines

www.boardreader.com-message boards

www.compinfo-center.com - computer information

www.completeplanet.com - get access here to over 100000 databases.

www.invisible-web.net - public records

www.itools.com - speech and language tools such as translators

www.laso.com - pop up maps displaying queries for hotels, and businesses

www.magportal.com - archives of magazine articles

www.researchville.com - search braking news from news organizations

www.singingfish.com - int. sources for all sorts of audio and video clips

switchboard.com - great source for finding people and places

www.infobel.com/teldir/ - many links to yellow pages, white pages, e-mail address and fax numbers

www.findsounds.com - helps you to locate sound files and includes a free audio player

RECREATION AND ENTERTAINMENT
General:

www.broadway.com - half price and discount tickets to shows

www.audible.com/adbl/store/ - a great source for books on tape with 20,000 selections *www.rubikscubes.com* - online version of the game

www.boxerjam.com - one of the oldest game sites on the Net featuring game shows, word games, and puzzles

imdb.com - Internet Movies Database

Shopping

ebay.com - famous for its auctions

amazon.com - one of the better e-commerce sites

shopping.yahoo.com - great for comparison-shopping

mysimon.com - another great site for comparison-shopping

epinions.com - reviews and prices

pricegrabber.com - product comparisons, specs, and reviews

nextag.com - price comparisons (including taxes and shipping from online stores

techbargains.com - bargains in tech products

bizrate.oom - very comprehensive selections, reviews, and store ratings

dealtime.com - includes specs and availability of merchandise from vendors

Trains and Train Museums

www.kalmbach.com - kalmbach publishing: The annual guide to Tourist Railroads and Museums

www.railwaymuseums.org - Association of Railway Museums

www.trains.org - Tourist Railway Organization

routesinternational.com - click on museum link for worldwide listing of hundreds of rail museums

TRAVEL

General Reference:

myboomerang.org - links for boomers to local resources, lifelong learning, volunteering, wellness

elderhostel.org - programs in 30 countries

www.montanarailtours.com - Montana Daylight Train Tours

www.virtualrelocation.com - describes many communities

tandemclub.org- ideas for bicycle tours

santanainc.com - bicycle manufacturer that sponsors worldwide tours

www.disneyworld.com - Disney World

www.hiayh.org - Hostelling International

nationalparks.org - If you're over 62, sign up for a lifetime pass here for only $10 *www.franceguide.com* - a guide to vacationing in Paris

www.roadfood.com - "Eat Your Way Across America", a review of hundreds of restaurants and diners around the US

www.vegetarian-vacations.com - a site devoted to vacations for veggie people

www.walkingtheworld.com - worldwide walking vacations

geox.com - walking and hiking trips to exotic destinations

seniorcycling.com - bike vacations for the over 50 population

eurobike.com - specializes in bike and hike vacations

eldertreks.com - over 50 land and marine vacations

fodors.com - a plethora of travel information

frommers.com - a popular travel name

Travel Deals

expedia.com - Microsoft enterprise

hotwire.com

cheaptickets.com

luxury-hotels-resorts.com/

travelocity.com - offers e-mail link to let you know when fares drop

orbitz.com

travel.yahoo.com - Yahoo Travel

valuevoyager.com - a terrific source for cruise deals

cruise.com - cruise deals

ncl.com - Norwegian Cruise Lines

royalcaribbean.com - Royal Caribbean Cruise Lines

offpeaktravel.com - offers big savings for off-peak travelers

cheaprooms.com

cheapfares.com

priceline.com - bid on what you'd like to pay

bestfares.com

site59.com - last minute travel deals

onetravel.com - international travel fares

seatguru.com - advice about airplane seating

seatexpert.com - same as above

budgettravel.msnbc.com - Frommer's budget travel guide

Traveling With Grandchildren

rascalsinparadise.com - travel agency specializing in traveling with kids

grandtravel.com - offers a variety of luxury tours with a focus on natural attractions and historical sites

elderhostel.org - grandtravel program provides links to worldwide travel opportunities with kids

Finding the Best Beaches

travel.discovery.com/convergence/beachweek/interactives/
americas.html - Travel Channel rates the best beaches
bestbeaches.org - best beaches on the southwest coast of Florida
bugbog.com - best beaches in the world
petrix.com/beaches - Dr. Stephen Leatherman ranks beaches and offers pictures

Travel Forums: Timely Advice

thorntree.lonelyplanet.com - thousands of new postings each day
groups.google.com - type in "rec.travel"
virtualtourist.com - lots of tourist tips

Vacation Property Rentals

www.a1vacations.com - over 5000 vacation property rentals around the world with descriptions and photos
www.vacationhomes.com
www.escapehomes.com
www.cyberrentals.com
vacationrentalguides.com

mountain-home.com - rental listings in Montana

resortquest.com - property management listing services

www.choice1.com - listing service with excellent search mechanism

vrma.com - Vacation Rental Managers Association

House Swapping Agencies

www.homelink.org - HomeLink (800-638-38410), $50 annual fee to list, around 12000 listings worldwide

www.homeexchange.com - HomeExchange.com (800-898-9660), strong in the area of domestic listings, 5000 listings in the US, $50 annual fee to list

www.ihen.com - International Home Exchange Network (386-238-3633) strong in the area of domestic listings, 2000 listings in the US, $29 to list

intrervac.org - Intervac US (800-756-4663) a worldwide organization devoted to house swapping. All details are provided for. Many countries in the free world are listed. $50 annual fee to list

trading-homes.com - offers virtual tours of properties, yearly fee sixty-five dollars, boast great customer service

Motorhome Rentals

cruiseamerica.com - domestic motorhome rentals

www.elmonte.com - domestic motorhome rentals

omtinc.com - overseas motorhome rentals

tracksrvtours.com - complete motorhome rental and vacation packages with everything included.

RV Travel

rvia.com - National RV Industry Association

rvtraderonline - a source to buy used RVs

rvsearch.com - another source to buy used RVs

www.rvnet.com - a source for clubs and other timely advice

www.movinon.net - advice for full time Rvers by the Hofmeisters

www.goodsamclub.com - a very complete RV club

rvusa.com/rvmanuf.asp - a list of RV manufacturers to obtain literature

rversonline.com - a good source for used RV inspection tips

nadaguides.com - provides values for used RVs

Tourist Train Travel

Loglink.net/tourtrains.htm - listings of tourist trains

traintraveling.com/usa - links to tourist trains by state including itinerary descriptions and prices

routesinternational.com/touristtrains.htm - worldwide alphabetical listing of tourist railways and other related sites

SPORTING ACTIVITIES

redsox.com - Home of the Boston Red Sox. You can read about and buy tickets to most sporting events by simply replacing the "redsox" id with the team you are looking for.

espn.com - scores and commentary

GOVERNMENT

thomas.loc.gov - a one stop site for government information

spaceflight.nasa.gov - history of space flight

firstgov.gov - the federal government's official web portal

pueblo.gsa.gov/call - federal citizen information center

HOBBIES

General

google.com - type in "hobbies A-Z" for extensive resources

retirementwithapurpose.com/hobbies - offers links on many hobbies

Antiques

antiqueweb.com - links to all types of collectibles and techniques

restoration-advice.org/ - features lots of tips on restoration

Art

Correspondence Schools:

detc.org - assistance on legitimacy of correspondence schools

www.artists-ais.com - Art Instruction Schools

www.newmasters.com - Gordon School of Art

masterclassstudios.com - Master Class studios

Online Courses:

aionline.edu - Art Institute Online

newschool.edu - Parsons School of Design

mcad.edu - Minneapolis College of Art and Design

mica.edu - Maryland Institute College of Art

Limited Residency Programs:

mcgregor.edu - Antioch University McGregor

meca.edu - Maine College of Art

syr.edu - Syracuse University Graduate School

Classic Cars

classiccarclub.org - Classic Car Club of America

classiccar.com

buyclassiccars.com

hemmings.com - Hemmings Motor News

Technology

pcworld.com - reviews of technology tools and strategies

macworld.com - same as above for Mac

www.annoyances.org - a trusted source for Windows information with a great glossary and Windows roadmap.

www.dotphoto.com - a free photo service that allows you to make online photo albums with sound clips.

hardcop.com - over clock watcher for PC owners

www.driverguides.com - 70,000 downloadable drivers for Windows

www.animfactory.com - 150000 animations and 3000 animated gifs for web pages

www.pcpitstop.com - web based tune up for your PC

pcworld.com/downloads - free downloads from PC World

Home Improvements

popularmechanics.com - reviews of vehicles, electronics, home improvements

bhg.com - online version of Better Homes and Gardens

hgtv.com - Home and Garden TV with links to This Old House tips

Gardening

www.garden.org - Official site of the National Gardening Association

gardenweb.com - online meetinghouse to swap tips

www.gardenguides.com - fact pact tip sheets with over 170 links

www.thegardenhelper.com - advice from a garden guru

www.plantcare.com - an extensive alphabetical list

www.bhg.com - online version of Better Homes and Gardens

www.hort.net - quick course in plant information

hgtv.com - Home and Garden TV Network

Investing and Financial Matters

morningstar.com

vanguard.com

smartmoney.com

www.thestreet.com

www.cbsmarketwatch.com

finance.yahoo.com

fidelity.com

irs.gov - for tax implications

www.better-investing.org - help in forming investment clubs (National Association of Investors Corp.)

www.fool.com - The Motley Fool financial site

chickslayingnesteggs.com - investment clubs for women

aadmm.com - web site of the American Association of Daily Money Managers, which offers personal assistance with financial tasks

Yoga

yogasite.com - great yoga resource directory

www.yogajournal.com - yoga updates

Tai Chi

www.taichi.com - information on the art of Tai Chi

Hiking

www.gorp.org - great hiking resource with maps and gear discussions

www.outdoors.org - Appalachian Mountain Club

Biking

www.tandemclub.org - Tandem Bicycle Club of America

www.santanainc.com - manufacturer's site with great tips and trips

ecycletours.com - Erickson Bicycle Tours

Walking and General Exercise

justwalk.com - record keeping for weight loss and goals

walkingvacations.com - an assortment of walking vacations

firstpath.com - fitness calculators

discoverfitness.com - tips for exercise motivation

zapfitness.com - illustrates running camps and exercise testing

Cooking

foodtv.com - the TV food network with advice from chefs

www.bhg.com -Better Homes and Gardens Magazine

www.meals.com - lots of recipes and advice

www.epicurious.com

cooking.com - much professional information and advice

Astronomy

www.hubble.stsci.edu - captured images by the Hubble telescope

Genealogy

www.genealogy.com - a great way to begin a family tree

www.genhomepage.com - a site loaded with great links

www.genealogy.org - RootsWeb database

www.jewishgen.org - home of Jewish genealogy

familytreemagazine.com - assistance in discovering family history

Great Museums

www.louvre.fr - Le Louvre art museum in Paris

VOLUNTEER ORGANIZATIONS

aarp.org- volunteer links

score.org- Service Corps. Of Retired Executives

www.iesc.org - International Executive Service Corps

literacyvolunteers.org - Literacy Volunteers of America

servenet.org – list of volunteer organizations

volunteermatch.org - matches your needs with agencies

bbsa.org - Big Brother/Big Sisters of America

seniorcorps.org - Senior Corps (Foster Grandparent Program)

nps.gov/volunteer - volunteering in our National Park system

habitat.org - Habitat for Humanity

www.peacecorps.gov - The Peace Corps

www.americorps.gov - the domestic partner of the Peace Corps

www.globalvolunteers.org - global Volunteers of America

eldercraftsmen.org - organization for elder craftsmen who would like to volunteer

mowaa.org - Meals on Wheels of America

unitedway.org - United Way of America

vfp.org - lists many International Workcamps for volunteers

voa.org - Volunteers of America with links to local affiliates

nationalservice.org - National Service Corps.

easi.org - recruits and trains seniors for environmental projects

EDUCATION

Distance Learning

www.dir.yahoo.com/Education/Distance_Learning - Yahoo directory of Distance Learning

www.GetEducated.com - distance learning consulting company, which also offers a free distance learning publication, entitled " The Best Distance Learning Education Schools"

www.uponline.com - University of Phoenix Online

Theme Cruises (Learn While Having Fun)

raddison7seas.com - Raddison Seven Seas

crystalcruises.com - Crystal Cruises

sailmainecoast.com - Maine Windjammer Association

deltaqueen.com - Delta Queen Steamboat Company

cunnard.com - Cunnard Company (Queen Elizabeth Two)

Learning a New Language (on location)

www.ecuadorbeach.com/spanish_school/ - Canoa Spanish Language School in Ecuador

eduamazonas.com/ - Spanish immersion language school in Ecuador

scuolaleondardo.com – Italian Language School

SUGGESTED READING

Adventure of Retirement, by Guild Fetridge, (Prometheus Books, $9.00), explores behavioral, emotional, and lifestyles issues related to retirement.

Virtues of Aging, by Jimmy Carter, (Ballantine Publishing, $9.95), The former President offers his perspective on making the most of aging and retirement.

It's Only too late If You Don't Start Now, by Barbara Sher, (Delacorte Press, $22.95). The author presents a Positive approach on entering the "second life" with a new outlook on recapturing dreams.

Retire and Thrive, by Robert Otterbourg, (Kiplinger Books, $15). A group of interesting people shares their retirement strategies. This book also helps you assess your interests.

Get a Life-You Don't Need a Million to Retire Well, by Ralph Warner, (Nolo Press). The author justifies why certain activities are beneficial to you in retirement, Included are lots of financial suggestions.

What Do You Want to Do When You Grow Up? Starting the Next Chapter of Your Life, by Dorothy Cantor,(Little, Brown and Company). This is a book that is philosophical by nature with interviews of people who discuss their hopes and dreams. This is s helpful publication for mindset development.

How to Create Your Own Super Second Life What are you going to do with your extra 30 years? By Gordon Burgett (Communication Unlimited) If you need lists for planning, and taking stock of yourself, then this is the book for you. Includes 28 worksheets and forms and activity lists.

Purpose and Power in Retirement by Harold Koenig M.D., (Templeton Foundation Press, 2002)

Support Your RV Lifestyle! An Insiders Guide to Working on the Road by Jaime Hall (Pine Country Publishing, $19.95) Mrs. Hall and her husband lived on the road for eight years. In the book she identifies more than 300 ways to make a living on the road and gives advice how to land a job.

And Thou Shalt Honor: The Caregivers Companion by Beth McLeod, (Rodale Books) Specific advice is offered to caregivers.

Ageless Body, Timeless Mind by Deepak Chopra, presents advise on slowing down the ageing process.

Retirement on a Shoestring by John Howells, (Globe Peqout Press) A wide variety of advice on all aspects of retirement including relocation, financial matters, and working.

The Grown-Up's Guide to Retiring Abroad by Rosanne Knorr, (Ten Speed Press) Very comprehensive guide to retiring abroad with discussions including taxes, weather, cost of living, health care, advantages and disadvantages and education.

Retirement Careers by Deloss L. Marsh, (Williamson Publishing) a helpful guide in the retiree's attempt to get a desirable job, with advice on resume preparation, developing the appropriate work attitude, and finding a balance between work and leisure.

50 Fabulous Places to Retire in America by Lee and Saralee Rosenberg, (Career Press) a complete profile accompanies each recommended area, tips included on how to prepare for retirement, also financial planning advice is in the book along with most appropriate snapshot data for the area.

Authentic Happiness - Using the New Positive Psychology to Realize Your Potential For Lasting Fulfillment, by Martin Seligman, Ph.D, (Free Press, 2002)- This book provides practical psychological wisdom which promotes happiness, inspiration, and mental, moral and spiritual well-being, also includes advice on renewing personal strength in an effort to be optimistic about the future.

Don't Retire, REWIRE! By Jeri Sedlar and Rick Miners, (Alpha Publishers, 2003), a broad perspective offered for the many people who would prefer not to stop working after retirement, but rather would prefer to rewire (find something personally and financially rewarding), discussions of part-time work, second careers, and volunteering ensue, along with advice of how to setup an action plan.

Finding Flow, by Mihaly Csikszentmihalyi, (BasicBooks, 1997), an inspirational book that encourages self-fulfillment, focused energy in the form of flow eliminates passive leisure time and makes the individual more productive by utilizing the opportunities of leisure.

The New Retirement, by Jan Cullinane and Cathy Fitzgerald, (Rodale Press, 2004), an updated general information book that discusses how to assess your estate and making your money last, as well as expatriation, travel, working options, and much more.

Retiring As a Career, by Betsy Kyte Newman, (Praeger, 2003), a good resource that helps to set up a psychological framework for the retiree, with discussion of various roles and resources for the individual, and deals with issues of self esteem and emotional and social roles; a good book to help you set up that all important plan.

Looking Forward: An Optimist's Guide to Retirement, by Ellen Freudenheim, (Stewart, Tabori, and Chang, 2004), a general reference guide to prepare potential retirees for a period of reinvention; informative text discusses why a retiree would get involved in various activities and includes suggested resources for those activities.

The Power Years, by Ken Dychtwald, and Daniel J. Kadlec, (Wiley & Sons, 2005), a general resource guidebook that encourages the reader to realize his potential with an emphasis on reinvention after the age of forty, the reader is shown how to rekindle passions and rediscover relationships and find a balance between work and leisure.